WHY

SO

DEPRESSED

Debi Pryde

Iron Sharpeneth Iron Publications
Newberry Springs, California

The Ironwood Toolbook Series

The Ironwood Toolbook Series is designed to address specific facets of ministry and to provide practical instruction in areas such as leadership, management, counseling, team building, youth work, music, and service ministries. The tried and tested contents of this series, an integral part of Ironwood, are now available to assist individuals and ministries. To God alone be the glory for the countless hours of service that have made this series possible.

Unless otherwise noted, Scripture quotations are from the Authorized King James Version.

For information concerning the Ironwood Toolbook Series or any other resources listed in this book, contact us at www.ironwood.org.

Managing Editor, Shannon B. Steuerwald
Cover Design, Susanna I. Capetz
Content Layout, Allison Pust

Iron Sharpeneth Iron Publications
Newberry Springs, California

TABLE OF CONTENTS

WHY AM I
SO
Depressed

PART ONE

.

DOES JESUS *Care?*

CHAPTER ONE

T wo friends sat at a restaurant table casually discussing the problem of depression. The first friend embarked on a lengthy description and then began to discuss, in clinical language, all the latest conflicts and disagreements concerning depression. The other friend, sitting across from her, sighed deeply and in exasperation abruptly interrupted, "I KNOW what depression is like—I'm living it! And I don't care what all the different kinds of depressions are called. I just want to know how this black cloud took over my life and how I can become normal again!"

Perhaps some can identify with the sentiments of this young woman who simply wanted answers, not a clinical description of her agony or the latest statistics. There might be some who are weary of advice or therapy that ignores the Bible and never mentions its significance in the matter. Or worse, others may have encountered someone who has mis-used the Bible or misrepresented the tender mercies of the Lord Jesus Christ. Perhaps some are seeking help for a friend or loved one who is caught in the confusing maze of depression and can't seem to find his or her way out. The following information is written specifically for those who long for compassion and truth and at the same time are ready to open the Bible to examine what it has to say about depression and the solutions God offers to believers who suffer.

Begin Where God Begins

The sincere Christian who is looking for answers and godly direction consistent with the Word of God must first begin with the Bible. Does God really care or have compassion for those who are so fragile they seem ready to break with the least bit of rough handling? Does He have anything specific to say about the kind of sorrow and incapacitating discouragement that is the experience of those who are depressed? Does the Bible give any kind of direction to those whose suffering is caused by physical illness? Most importantly, does He offer a way of escape from depression and hope for renewed joy and peace?

Before proceeding to discuss various causes of depression and specific ways to deal with it, one must be assured that the heart of God is touched with our grief and extends love and mercy to those who are drowning in a sea of hopelessness. He *does* address this common human problem, and He does have a lifeline that can pull the weary believer in from the storm and set him on a solid rock.

Jesus' Response to Depression

Throughout Jesus' life on earth, He spoke to those who were sorrowful with compassion and gentleness. God tells us in *Matthew 12:20* that "a bruised reed shall he not break, and smoking flax shall he not quench..." Jesus sharply rebuked those whose hearts were hardened and proud, but He never spoke a harsh word to those who were broken and seeking His help. Jesus assures us that, "...him that cometh to me I will in no way cast out" (*John 6:37*). Jesus is described as a good and loving shepherd throughout the Scriptures, but perhaps no other passage paints the tender picture of Christ's relationship to His own as well as the description in *Isaiah 40:11*. "He shall feed his flock like a shepherd: he shall gather the lambs with his arm, and carry them in his bosom, and shall gently lead those that are with young." There is something very touching in seeing Christ, the strong and powerful Creator God, as a kind and caring Shepherd, stooping to gather a helpless little lamb in His arms or slowing down in order to gently lead a pregnant ewe. What sensitivity and compassion!

Jesus Himself suffered grief and, in fact, was called a "man of sorrows" (*Isaiah 53:11; Matthew 26:37-44; Mark 14:34-42; Luke 22:42-44*). Job suffered grief and was never rebuked by God for his sorrow. The widow of Nain grieved for the loss of her son, and Jesus in compassion raised him from the dead. God noticed and expressed compassion for Hagar's sorrow (*Genesis 21:17-20*). He expressed compassion for Israel's sorrow (*Exodus 3:7-10*), for Hannah's sorrow (*1 Samuel 1:15*), for David's sorrow in the death of his infant son (*2 Samuel 12:16-23*), for Martha and Mary's sorrow (*John 11:19,40*), and for Jeremiah's sorrow (*Lamentations 1:12*). God instructs believers to compassionately "weep with those who weep" as He Himself does, not to rebuke them (*Romans 12:15*).

Our God invites us to call upon Him and rely on His mercy and love to lift us up from the sorrows that can so easily envelop us. David rejoiced as he discovered the blessings of trusting God and declared, "But thou, O Lord, art a shield for me; my glory, and the lifter up of mine head" (*Psalm 3:3*). Over and over David assures us of God's lovingkindness, mercy, and compassion. Over and over he praises the Lord for delivering him from tears and distress. "For thou hast delivered my soul from death, mine eyes from tears, and my feet from falling" (*Psalm 116:8*). How sweet are the promises we find in David's songs, for they comfort our hearts and give us courage to seek and trust the Lord as he did. "He healeth the broken in heart, and bindeth up their wound." (*Psalm 147:3*). "For he shall deliver the needy when he crieth; the poor also, and him that hath no helper" (*Psalm 72:12*).

Because Jesus clearly desires us to seek Him when we are overwhelmed and discouraged, we can rest assured that He will not turn us away. Regardless of why we are feeling despair and no matter what the process of overcoming it, the first step will always be to call on the Lord. He alone knows exactly what is causing the difficulty, and He alone knows us better than we know ourselves. Jesus is called Wonderful Counselor, the Mighty God, the Everlasting Father, and the Prince of Peace. He is more than qualified to help us unravel the tangled cords of depression and invites us to call upon Him in the day of trouble. "And call upon me in the day of trouble: I will deliver thee, and thou shalt glorify me" (*Psalm 50:15*). Jesus speaks to those who have trusted Him as their Savior and says, "If ye continue in my word, then are ye my disciples indeed; and ye shall know the truth, and the truth shall make you free" (*John 8:31-32*). *If* means "provided that." *If* we continue in His Word, *then* we are true followers of Christ, and then we may claim the promise that we will know the truth and God's truth will set us free from whatever enslaves us and robs us of joy.

The Bible's Description of Depression

The same symptoms and manifestations of clinically defined depression are also described in the Bible. Although the King James Bible doesn't use the word *depression*, it does use terms such as "cast down," "sorrow," "overwhelmed in sorrow," "despair," "dis-contented," or "troubled." These are colorfully descriptive words that give us a window of understanding into the origins and nature of many kinds of depression. If we define depression as the Bible does, it would be most accurate to say that depression is, in general, "sorrow without hope." The Bible teaches that such a mental condition is often the reflection of a state of mind in which an individual focuses on real or imagined problems, difficulties, perils, or losses with a perspective of defeat and despair. When this occurs, it is more than sorrow—it is sorrow without hope. (Hope is a confident anticipation of God's promised good outcome.)

There are many passages that describe this kind of heart-wrenching agony of spirit. That it is a common human experience even among those who are regarded as our heroes of the faith is evident by the numerous passages that address the subject. Jesus, when comforting His disciples before His crucifixion offered words of hope intended to prepare them for one of the most devastating, confusing, and sorrowful times of their lives. He said, "And ye now therefore have sorrow: but I will see you again, and your heart shall rejoice, and your joy no man taketh from you" (*John 16:22*). The mighty king David, having been unjustly mistreated and betrayed by friends, describes his hopeless mental state. He cried out to God, "Save me, O God; for the waters are come in unto my soul. I sink in deep mire, where there is no standing; I am come into deep waters, where the floods overflow me. I am weary of my crying: my throat is dried: mine eyes fail while I wait for my God" (*Psalm 69:1-3*).

Jeremiah felt as if his whole world had come unraveled and his life had become enveloped in one huge cloud of darkness. In *Lamentations 3* he described his fear that God had forsaken him. He told of his lack of direction, physical brokenness, isolation, hopelessness, confusion, desolation, rejection, and humiliation. Only when the prophet recalled God's comforting words of hope did he find reassurance and conclude, "It is of the Lord's mercies that we are not consumed, because his compassions fail not. They are new every morning; great is thy faithfulness. The Lord is my portion, saith my soul; therefore will I hope in him" (*Lamentations 3:21-24*).

Elijah knew moments where he wished he were dead and was so depleted of hope that he requested God take his life. We read in *1 Kings 19:4*, "But he himself went a day's journey into the wilderness, and came and sat down under a juniper tree; and he requested for himself that he might die; and said, It is enough; now O Lord, take away my life; for I am not better than my fathers." At that moment, Elijah was both physically and mentally exhausted, depleted of all physical and spiritual strength. Yet in tenderness the Lord let him sleep until he was refreshed, and then sent an angel to prepare food for him and encourage him to go on. Once physically strengthened, God led him to a quiet place in the wilderness where Elijah continued to speak with the pessimistic outlook of depression. He tells God, "...I, even I only, am left; and they seek my life, to take it away" (*1 Kings 19:14b*). The Lord's rebuke was gentle, and His questions designed to provoke Elijah to rethink from a perspective other than his own. God then simply gave him instructions for his next heavenly mission and said, "Go!" Elijah's mind was directed away from himself and his emotions and toward meaningful work. Evidently Elijah's perspective and confidence in God's protection was turned around, for he went on to serve with remarkable faith and courage and once again saw God's power and miracles demonstrated through his life.

These and many other passages give us little vignettes that beautifully and accurately describe the experience of depression. In them we see human weakness in the strongest of men, but just as clearly, the gentle strength and compassion of God as He restores hope to those whose hearts are broken and sorrowful. These descriptions, and many other passages of Scripture like them, give us the confidence that God does directly speak to the problem of depression many believers face today.

Personalities and Depression

Believers especially cherish *Psalm 139*, for in it David expresses his wonder and amazement concerning God's intimate knowledge and understanding of his individual personality and inborn characteristics. To think that the God of the universe knows us thoroughly as individuals and understands every thought in our heart and every pattern of behavior unique to our personality is beyond our comprehension. Yet the Bible repeatedly declares this to be so. David marvels that God knows him and thinks about him as an individual and exclaims, "How precious also are thy thoughts unto me, O God! How great is the sum of them!" (*verse 17*). The entire Psalm praises God for His love and care in the creation of every living soul; however, in *verse 3* David makes the statement that God is "thoroughly acquainted with all my ways." What an astounding thought—that God knows our ways.

We learn much about God's character by observing His creation, including human beings. Diversity and variety abound in every aspect of creation. The varieties of plant life and animals that exist in our world are simply amazing. Even the stars are individually numbered by God and called by name. It should not surprise us then, that God creates individuals who are unique as much as they are alike, rather than people who are exact duplicates of another. Each of us has patterns of behavior and ways that are as uniquely our own as are our fingerprints. In every generation, God uses men and women of every personality, ability and race. He gives each local church a variety of members, each possessing talents and abilities particularly suited to the work God has for each of His children to do.

We are blessed when we learn to appreciate the different ways God has created us and recognize that every kind of personality is needful in the body of Christ. Some personalities are better suited to teaching, others to serving behind the scenes or tending to the sick or weakened among us. Some personalities shine best in areas of financial disbursement while others blossom in areas of leadership. Without a doubt, personalities gravitate toward activities and areas of expression that differ from others. Certainly, we are created differently so that we are equipped to happily fulfill differing places of service to God. Yet with our differences in the area of personality also come differences in our weaknesses and vulnerabilities. Take-charge people who excel in leadership have more of a tendency to be overbearing and insensitive toward people's emotional states. People who are extroverted and excel in people skills add life to any gathering and put everyone at ease, but also tend to struggle in areas of impulsiveness. Contemplative people are indispensable as problem solvers and organizers, yet are often more prone to being observers than participators.

Then there are the artistic folks. They are people who are naturally sensitive toward subtle changes and differences in everything from sound to color. They are the artists, musicians, and writers who seem to thrive best when they are utilizing their innovative skills and sensitive natures in a variety of expressive ways. Yet this personality too, has corresponding weaknesses. The "artistic" personality is not only sensitive to beauty and joy; it is sensitive toward disharmony and the darker emotions as well. The lows tend to be lower than most, and the highs higher than average. Artistic people are especially tempted to follow their emotions and feelings rather than objective facts, and they have a strong tendency towards introverted thinking and over analyzing. Because depression tends to thrive and grow best in the soil of a contemplative mind that is easily influenced by emotions, this personality faces a far greater danger of becoming ensnared by it. Some believe that this type of personality has the greatest potential to excel and succeed in life, but along with it, the greatest vulnerability to discouragement, self-pity, and despair. Certainly, to the degree such a person is able to recognize both his strengths and weaknesses and will discipline his mind accordingly, is the degree to which he will be able to use his particular God-given talents in constructive and rewarding ways.

With or Without Him

The very first person a depressed believer needs to call upon when he finds himself struggling with the temptation to lose hope is the Lord. Regardless of the underlying causes of depression, God is a believer's Rock and Refuge. It is He Who orders the steps of every redeemed child of God and He alone Who knows all the reasons and ways a person's experience with depression will be used for good. Apart from Him, there is no cure for any problem or illness. Doctors who treat illness with medical intervention usually are a blessing, but even they are subject to the sovereign work of God. Alone, a person is without hope or resources. With Him, a person may confidently say, "I can do all things through Christ which strengtheneth me" (*Philippians 4:13*). A struggling believer must not imagine he is capable of resolving life's difficulties apart from God's provisions and mercy, no matter what the difficulty is. Understanding this truth, a believer then understands that prayer is where the journey begins in order to return to joy and peace.

God has a specific order—first we step out in faith and call upon our God, then He sends His Word, then we respond in obedience, then He delivers us from trouble. "And call upon me in the day of trouble: I will deliver thee, and thou shalt glorify me" (*Psalm 50:15*). "Then they cry unto the Lord in their trouble, and he saveth them out of their distresses. He sent His word, and healed them, and delivered them from their destructions" (*Psalm 107:19-20*). A person is not to behave as though he were in this trial alone or as if the Captain of the host is not leading the way through the battle. The Christian is to seek God first, knowing God is intimately involved with his life and has in His hand the power to bless and heal, or not bless and heal—with or without the experts.

King Asa failed to recognize God's merciful providential work in allowing him to suffer illness in order to turn him back to a life of trust and fellowship with God as he once experienced in his younger years. Instead of adjusting his priorities, or submitting his hardened will to God in humility and adoration, he ignored God completely, as if God did not matter, and turned to doctors for a cure. Consulting with physicians was not Asa's sinful error. His sin was in consulting physicians without consulting with God, without putting His trust in God, and without acknowledging that God alone gives power to heal, whether He chooses to use medicine, supernatural means, the body's own defenses, or something else of His own choosing. Asa clearly trusted in the power and reasoning of man alone apart from God—and it cost him his life. The Scriptures tell us that in the thirty-ninth year of Asa's reign he was diseased in his feet, "until his disease was exceeding great: yet in his disease he sought not to the Lord, but to the physicians. And Asa slept with his fathers, and died..." (*2 Chronicles 16:12-13*).

God does use people and means, but many err as Asa did by ignoring the fact that God is intimately involved in the lives of His own children. He is not only the Almighty Creator God, but the Good Shepherd Who governs and oversees every minor or major thing that takes place in the lives of His own. It is crucial for the child of God to seek the Lord and put his trust in Him alone before he embarks on a journey for answers and help with the problem of depression. David himself experienced the same sorrows and tenacious grip of depression that many people today may experience, yet he assures us, "The Lord also will be a refuge for the oppressed, a refuge in times of trouble. And they that know thy name will put their trust in thee: for thou, Lord, hast not forsaken them that seek thee" (*Psalm 9:9-10*). And again we are both instructed and comforted by David's prayer, "Be merciful unto me, O God, be merciful unto me; for my soul trusteth in thee: yea, in the shadow of thy wings will I make my refuge, until these calamities be overpast. I will cry unto God most high; unto God that performeth all things for me" (*Psalm 57:1-2*).

DEPRESSION'S

Origin

T he medical labels often given to those who suffer depression confuse many believers. Many wonder if the labels are valid, or they wonder if a depressed person suffers from some kind of physical illness. Others reject the idea that depression can *ever* have a purely biological origin and therefore, avoid medical doctors altogether when they or a loved one becomes consumed in melancholy or disoriented thinking. Before we can clear up some of this confusion or know how to apply specific biblical principles to our problem, we must first understand a little about the physiological connection between depression and illness.

That depression affects us physically is not in question. Without a doubt, all emotions have a corresponding physical effect in our bodies and prolonged emotions such as sadness, fear, or anger *do* deplete our physical strength and cause many well-documented physical problems as well as chemical changes. Sorrow is capable of interfering with a person's normal ability to function and can interrupt sleep, change one's eating hab-

17

its, zap all normal desires for social or physical interaction, and almost nullify one's ability to concentrate and fulfill daily responsibilities. The real question that is often completely ignored or avoided is this: which comes first, the physical change in body chemistry, or the sadness and other symptoms that are associated with it?

Two Classifications of Depression

The majority of all depressions treated by medical professionals are classified as *reactive*. In other words, the depression obviously developed in *response* to events that have taken place in a person's life or in response to how he reacted to the events. In reactive depression, the *origin* of the debilitating depression and discouragement begins in one's thought processes and perception of loss or rejection or some other traumatic event. What follows is a very real change in bodily functions that set off a chain of physiological responses that further complicate the suffering. When the circumstantial problem is resolved or thinking is restored to normal, the body gradually follows a return to normal functioning as well.

A very common form of reactive depression begins when a physiological change, such as fatigue or a woman's monthly cycle, produces low feelings or mild depression that are misinterpreted as abnormal. People who are not sufficiently distracted with productive activity or who are sensitive to subtle changes in their mood very often attach more significance to the emotional low than is warranted. Instead of accepting and ignoring this kind of melancholy, they frequently assume their depression is caused by something they are unhappy about, which prompts introspective thinking and dwelling on real, but small problems that would not usually cause concern. What initially may have begun as a normal physiological low quickly spirals into full-fledged depression. Little problems and irritations suddenly become overwhelming and melancholy feelings cloud sound judgment and wreak havoc with emotions. In many cases, once the underlying physical trigger to this sequence of events subsides, emotions and a positive outlook on life abruptly return, leaving the sufferer somewhat bewildered by his or her brief episode with depression.

Depression is often a reaction, but it can also be a *symptom* of a physical problem that does *not* originate in one's response to life circumstances. Diseases of the pituitary gland or thyroid are able to cause depression. Extreme physical exhaustion is capable of producing depression as well as female hormone changes, diabetes, brain tumors, Lyme disease, and various other common illnesses. Some people become depressed when they are fighting an infection, the flu, or a bout with asthma. Others experience mild to severe depression as a side effect of various prescription drugs, including those prescribed for high blood pressure, contraception, or heart arrhythmias. Depression caused by physiological changes and problems may be mild to severe. Mild depression associated with a temporary physiological change may actually serve a good purpose, such as slowing a person down so he can recover from an illness, sparking more innovative activity, or alerting him that something is wrong. In some instances, medical intervention may be as simple as encouraging the patient to engage in more physical exercise so that the body will naturally produce the chemicals needed to maintain a sense of well-being. Changes in diet, medications, sleep habits, or daily routines may be all that is needed to dramatically lift many kinds of depression.

Treating Depression

Regardless whether the depression is reactive or symptomatic of illness, a person needs to accurately treat the underlying problem or problems that are producing the depression if the depression is to be overcome. The process of discovering an underlying cause should begin with a thorough medical examination in order to identify or eliminate physical problems as a precipitating factor. In the small minority of cases, medical tests will confirm the depression has an organic basis that is purely physiological in origin. These situations require professional medical treatment from those who understand the medical problem and are able to treat it effectively through the use of medicine or medical intervention. Very often a doctor will recommend that such a patient seek additional counseling in order to help him cope with physical difficulties and respond to illness in ways that will minimize emotional impact and corral runaway emotions. In the vast majority of depressions, however, the origin will be found to have its roots in the way one reacts and thinks.

Many people would prefer to hear that their depression has a physiological basis that is completely unassociated with the way they respond to circumstances. A disease may seem easier to resolve or more attractive than something involving one's volition or thought processes. In many cases, depressed individuals refuse to consider any possibility other than a biological origin and sometimes go to great lengths to prove it is so even in the absence of any pathological evidence to support such a theory. Plenty of doctors have no problem appeasing such patients with anti-depressants, anti-anxiety medications, or an endless supply of muscle relaxants and sleep aids. These treatments may help patients find a measure of relief either in the medication itself or simply in receiving a response that appears to confirm their hopes. What medication doesn't do is accurately identify or resolve the underlying problem.

Believers who understandably long for relief often fall prey to every imaginable sort of explanation or regimen that promises a cure. There is no lack of people crouched to exploit the depressed in order to sell their particular product or point of view. Depression is big business, whether it is for drug companies, publishers of self-help books, clinics that thrive on insurance claims, alternative medicine gurus, or the like. Though many suggestions and treatments may not be harmful and some even helpful, none brings believers any closer to resolving the real problem unless the suggestions and treatments offer hope and solutions that are freely provided in the Bible. Problems that do not have a medical origin will not be resolved by any kind of medical intervention. Medicine may relieve symptoms, and in some cases this is helpful, but it does not heal a wounded heart or correct an underlying cause. Similarly, treating medically-based depression as a spiritual problem or a dietary problem is likewise ineffective.

Ignoring the origin of depression or explaining it away with a false assumption may initially "feel" better or seem more palatable, but in the long run, it prevents real healing and personal growth. In a similar way, taking pain relievers for a severely abscessed tooth may seem preferable over root canal surgery; however, pain pills only treat the symptoms while root canal surgery treats the underlying cause. Gaining relief from pain through the use of drugs only prolongs the problem and suppresses it—drugs do not resolve the problem. To be sure, pain pills have their place and are certainly capable of bringing temporary relief. They simply cannot provide long term relief, nor do they eradicate the inevitable need for surgery. Treating symptoms without treating causes will only acerbate the problem further.

When no precipitating biological cause is discovered, the wise and humble believer will turn his attention toward other possibilities. In many cases, a skillful biblical counselor or pastor will be best suited to help a suffering believer discover exactly what it is in one's thought processes and responses that produce severe discouragement and mental anguish. A host of possibilities might be considered. For instance, some (but certainly not all) of the most common causes are a loss of hope when facing difficult circumstances, doubts concerning one's salvation, wrong assumptions about God and one's relationship to Him, introspective thinking habits, unresolved guilt, anger, jealousy, self-pity, or major disappointment. Because all of these difficulties are plainly addressed in the context of Scripture, the believer has sufficient resources to understand and overcome anything that might rob him of His joy and peace. Certainly, God does not abandon His sheep to wolves that are waiting to devour him. God is ever present and ready to protect, comfort, and guide His own. It makes no sense for a Christian to run from the One whose only interest is His child's welfare. As a child of God, Christians have full access to a loving Heavenly Father Who speaks soothing words of hope and direction.

Finding and removing the cause of *any* kind of depression is rarely easy or fast. Most of the time there are *several* underlying factors that contribute to the debilitating sadness and discouragement of depression. Therefore, there will also be several solutions. Certainly the careful believer is wise to seek medical attention in order to rule out physical causes of depression. At the same time, physical causes of depression. At the same time, one is *also* wise to seek out mature believers that will be able to minister encouragement and provide instruction in ways God has instructed us to do for one another.

What Causes Depression?

To make a sweeping pronouncement that all depression is the result of a lack of faith or an act of sin is a cruel and simplistic assumption that ignores the complexities of this very human experience and minimizes the realities of human suffering. Even when depression is the outcome of sinful behavior, it is the outcome of *specific* sinful behaviors, not the outcome of sin in general, and therefore requires specific applications of truth and understanding. Pinpointing spiritual error requires meticulous and careful thought, and cannot be accomplished without a considerable investment of time and effort. Those who give "one size fits all" answers typically do not fully understand the nature of this problem, or they often simply do not care to invest the time and compassion that is so necessary in individually sorting through the possibilities and particulars of one who is suffering. Nevertheless, while circumstances and particulars from one person to another might greatly vary, there *are* many general principles that are remarkably consistent in specific cases of depression.

Natural and Spiritual Laws

The problems of day-to-day living and the challenges of interacting with other people are circumstances all people are subject to in this life. The Scriptures say that all trials are universally common to man, and though experiences and reactions vary, they do contain certain dynamics that are common to man as well (*1 Corinthians 10:13*). God has set in place universal laws of physics to which every one is equally subject. People have a basic understanding of the laws of gravity, the laws of thermodynamics, and the laws of nature that are learned through experience or in school. From a person's earliest years he learns how such laws influence the outcome of choices to either respect or ignore them, and he learns how to live in such a way as to utilize these laws rather than be overcome by them. Knowing the forces of gravity, a person does not attempt to fly from a tree or climb up the side of a tall building. People intuitively learn how fast they can drive around a tight curve without losing control of a car or how far they can throw a ball before it lands on the ground. Accepting and understanding the laws God has put into place allows mankind to live within limitations and utilize them for his benefit.

Spiritual laws are as real as the unchangeable laws of nature that people are able to readily see and accept in the physical realm. All human beings are subject to the same basic limitations, capabilities, and consequences of violating God's spiritual laws. Because people are subject to the same dynamics in the spiritual or emotional realm, they are really very predictable when faced with a given set of circumstances. If this were not true, no one could instruct or guide another, let alone turn to the Bible for specific help and direction.

For instance, Christians know that the natural consequence of doubting God's love and shepherding care is a fear of God's judgment, according to *1 John 4:17-18* and other similar passages. Though some may have been raised in such a way that their confidence in God's love has matured and grown strong, other believers raised in different circumstances may struggle daily with doubts of God's love for them personally. Because the solution for this problem lies in the truth contained in the Bible and not a person's own personal experience, mature believers have the ability to encourage and convey to a struggling brother or sister in Christ the truth set forth in His Word. The Bible is God's gift to man, describing and illustrating the laws of human nature and laws in which God's Spirit moves. One may choose to ignore such spiritual laws or may simply remain unaware of them, yet he is still subject to them in the same way he is subject to the laws of nature. Depression cannot be resolved unless one is willing to examine laws of human nature in relationship to God and the laws of the Spirit that God has put in place.

God has made the human heart and body in such a way that a person experiences specific effects, both physical and spiritual, when he responds to life circumstances in different ways. For instance, in the physical realm, if one believes the large German shepherd walking toward him is a threat to his safety, he will automatically react with both voluntary and involuntary responses. He will voluntarily choose to walk on the other side of the street or go back into his house. His body will involuntarily begin to prepare itself to run or fight off the threat by pumping adrenaline into his system, increasing heart rate in order to pump oxygen to major body organs such as the heart and brain; and he will breathe more rapidly.

In the spiritual realm, a person experiences a sense of joy when he speaks graciously and kindly to others such as God promised in *Proverbs 15:23*, and guilt when he speaks sharply or impatiently. (See Application #9 entitled *My Part and God's Part*) His response may produce joy; or it may produce sorrow, depending on how he works with or against the unchangeable laws of God and human nature. One might think of it as a built-in system. Specific reactions produce specific, predictable results.

Depression is very often a result that stems from identifiable violations of the laws that govern every human life, whether a person is aware of what he is doing or whether he is not, whether a person is a believer, or whether a person does not believe or love God. For instance, *Jeremiah 17:5-8* contrasts the natural result of putting one's confidence in human ability rather than God. The life that depends on man is compared to a lone tumbleweed blowing aimlessly in a hot, barren desert where nothing green is flourishing. On the other hand, the person who has his trust in the Lord and has hope that is based in God's character and God's promises is compared to a large tree that is flourishing next to a flowing river. This tree has roots deeply anchored in the soil in every direction. As a result, the tree has no problem thriving even in the worst heat or drought, but goes on producing fruit without interruption. This is a picture of life, refreshment, productivity, and strength in contrast to the tumbleweed, which is a picture of something dead, unproductive, and tossed about with the slightest breeze. When the storms of life and times of drought come, the first man reacts by putting his trust in his or other's strength and ability. In the same storm, the second man reacts by putting his trust in God and has hope in God's truth. As a direct result of their reaction to trouble, the first man is cursed with despair, while the second man is blessed with joy. The Scriptures —
repeat this same spiritual law over and over as in *Proverbs 16:20*. "He that handleth a matter wisely shall find good; and whoso trusteth in the Lord, happy is he."

This is only one spiritual law that has a direct connection with to life circumstances that produce both joy and sorrow. The filled with many others. Work produces joy, while laziness p sorrow (*Psalm 128:2; Ecclesiastes 2:2; 3:13*). The quest for wisdom on God's terms results in joy, while a disinterest in God's wisdom leads to foolish behavior that produces sorrow (*Proverbs 3:13, 18*). The Bible tells us that those who react to a sinning neighbor with hatred rather than mercy experience sadness, while those who treat others with mercy have joy (*Proverbs 14:21; 21:15*). Over and over again the Bible shows how man's choices and reactions to life's circumstances and trials produce either joy or sorrow. (For more information on this topic, read *Secrets of a Happy Heart* by Debi Pryde.)

DEPRESSION
AS A
REACTION
TO
Loss

CHAPTER THREE

3

What the world labels as *depression* and what the Christian can more accurately call "sorrow without hope," should not be confused with genuine grief and sorrow over real loss, temporary uncertainty in a crisis, biological disturbances that adversely affect one's emotions, temporary disappointment, or the understandable frailty in human beings that causes them to feel a sense of hopelessness not warranted by the actual facts when faced with physical fatigue or real difficulties. Grief is a natural human response to loss, regardless whether one is saved or lost. It is an expression of one's longing to have restored that which has been lost. Grief might be a fleeting sadness or a complex reaction that envelops one's mind and emotions to such an extent that it brings one into the darkest valley of human experience. *It is not unspiritual or sinful to grieve or feel the painful emotions that accompany deep sorrow.*

Problems with grief intensify and spin out of control only when grief is not coupled with hope in God's mercy and care, or when it is not anchored in a confident faith that God will one day turn the sadness one experiences into joy when one trusts in God. Without an eternal perspective, grief turns into "sorrow without hope," or what is typically called, depression. Those who do not know the Lord Jesus as their Savior have no possibility for hope or faith in anything stable or unchangeable. There is no sturdy framework on which to build an unshakable faith and confidence in spite of life's inevitable disappointments and sorrows. As a result, they experience an intensity of sorrow and despair that believers do not need to experience (*1 Thessalonians 4:13*). Isaiah laments the hopeless despair of those who are lost. He said, "They that go down into the pit cannot hope for thy truth" (*Isaiah 38:18*).

Paul affirms that while trouble and persecutions are a normal part of living and bring with them a degree of sadness, the believer does not need to suffer trouble without assurance of God's purpose, or without available grace or strength to meet every need and trial. He reminds us that the believer's strength originates in the power of God within him, not in his own human abilities. Paul says, "But we have this treasure in earthen vessels, that the excellency of the power may be of God, and not of us" (*2 Corinthians 4:7*). God is said to be the "Father of mercies, and the God of all comfort who comforteth us in all our tribulation [trials]..." (*2 Corinthians 1:3-4*). Clearly, though afflictions and loss are common to everyone, the Christian is able to face them without overwhelming despair because he has resources the world does not. God never leaves His children alone and never forsakes them in times of affliction; no matter how much they may "feel" forsaken.

Paul, by inspiration of the Holy Spirit, wrote a wonderful antidote to sadness that might arise as a result of a loss of any sort. He does not minimize his own suffering nor deny that it is very real, but reports that when he views what he has lost in *comparison* to the things he has gained through his relationship with Christ, his losses are as insignificant as cow dung. Paul puts all of his losses into an eternal perspective in *Philippians 3:8-9* when he says, "Yea doubtless, and I count all things but loss for the excellency of the knowledge of Christ Jesus my Lord: for whom I have suffered the loss of all things, and do count them but dung, that I may win Christ, and be found in him, not having mine own righteous, which is of the law, but that which is through the faith of Christ, the righteousness which is of God by faith." This determination provides us with the key to why Paul could also say, "And the peace of God, which passeth all understanding, shall keep your hearts and minds through Christ Jesus" (*Philippians 4:7*).

Honestly facing and identifying the losses one experiences is an important part of adjusting one's thinking and accepting the "unchangeables" of life. Yet for the believer, it is far more than merely listing losses and calculating their impact on his life that brings one to a place of genuine peace. Peace comes only when such a process leads a believer to realign his priorities and move his attachment from the thing or person lost to the things of Christ and his personal relationship with Him, which can never be lost. A person will remain in torment of soul until he is willing to relinquish the thing or things lost into the care of He who is the Shepherd of man's souls—whether it be a reputation, a person, a relationship, possessions, a position, or hopes and dreams. All that would provide a person with security in this life must be relinquished to his Lord so that he might find true hope and security in Christ Himself. The main issue, then, is not the loss, but the significance one attaches to the loss and the context in which one views his losses.

A young woman living in relative poverty stumbled upon a beautiful piece of antique furniture at a garage sale. Because she enjoyed its beauty and unique characteristics, she scraped together enough money to buy it. After cleaning and polishing the piece, she displayed it in a prominent place in her home for several years and cared for it meticulously. The antique became such a favorite item that she decided that she would choose it as the one possession she would strive to save in the event of a house fire. Then one day, while watching a program on television that highlights antiques like hers, she heard that her rare piece was worth hundreds of thousands of dollars. She quickly investigated to learn if, in fact, she owned something this rare and valuable, ultimately discovering that indeed she did. As much as she admired the piece of furniture and enjoyed its beauty, she knew immediately that she would much rather have the five hundred thousand dollars that was being offered if she would sell it. It's not that she no longer enjoyed or valued the furniture, nor that it had no significance to her. She simply knew she would enjoy the money more and placed more importance on financial benefits than the pleasure of owning the beautiful piece of furniture. Given the choice, the money was of far greater value to her than the antique. Whereas before the antique would have caused her a great deal of disappointment had she lost it, now she gladly exchanges it for something she values more.

It is not sinful to value such things as good health, financial prosperity, comfort, talent, the love and esteem of others, the blessings of children, a loving spouse, or any other blessings such as these. However, when we value the rewards of suffering their loss for the cause of Christ more than we value the joys of material blessings, we exchange something that is precious for something that is of incomparable worth. Jesus told of a man who discovered a great treasure in a field being offered for sale. He quickly went home and sold everything he had in order to purchase that field. It wasn't that his things were of no value or their loss of no consequence. They simply were not as valuable as the field he wanted to buy. Again Jesus tells the story of a man who bought and sold beautiful and valuable pearls. One day he came across a pearl so beautiful and exquisite that he hurried home to sell everything he had in order to buy the precious pearl.

These illustrations are meant to help believers understand an important spiritual truth. The value a person attaches to something will determine what he does with or without it. First, one learns that the things of this world cannot be compared to the worth of finding salvation in Jesus Christ. Second, one is reminded that living for the pleasures found in this world is worthless in value *compared* to the pleasures that will be found in living for Christ and becoming more like Christ. Like Paul, every Christian is able to relinquish any pleasure found in this world in order to gain those things that are found in a relationship with Christ *when it is more valuable to the Christian to do so.* To the degree a person loves what he loses and believes he cannot be happy without it is the degree he will struggle if he does not exchange it for what he gains in

Christ. This pertains not only to the loss of possessions, but the loss of people or things we naturally hold dear, such as a beloved spouse who dies or abandons his family, a baby that is miscarried, a child that goes astray, an enjoyable job, friends that bring refreshment and fellowship, the respect of those esteemed, and so on.

Moses certainly experienced this human dilemma, and his was no easy exchange. "By faith, Moses, when he was come to years, refused to be called the son of Pharaoh's daughter; choosing rather to suffer affliction with the people of God, than to enjoy the pleasures of sin for a season; esteeming the reproach of Christ greater riches than the treasures in Egypt; for he had respect unto the recompense of the reward. By faith he forsook Egypt, not fearing the wrath of the king, for he endured, as seeing him who is invisible" (*Hebrews 11:23-27*).

Jesus' desire is to fill one's heart with His peace and His own joy, not to keep him from experiencing it. His written Word is full of wonderful words of comfort and reassurance. "Peace I leave with you, my peace I give unto you; not as the world giveth give I unto you. Let not your heart be troubled, neither let it be afraid" (*John 14:27*). Further on Christ says, "These things have I spoken unto you, that my joy might remain in you, and that your joy might be full" (*John 15:11*). Christ knew people would suffer sorrows and losses, and He knew people would experience times of perplexity when their heart's desires and expectations would seem to be senselessly withheld. In preparing Christians to live with a right perspective, He comforts His children by saying, "These things I have spoken unto you, that in me ye might have peace. In the world ye shall have tribulation: but be of good cheer; I have overcome the world" (*John 16:33*). Faulty perceptions to life's difficulties and imbalanced attachments to this life keep Christians from seeing the bigger picture of God's work in their lives, and the lives of others, and then rejoicing in the newly discovered joy and peace.

God's purpose for every believer is to bring him into right fellowship with God and to conform him from the inside out into a person who reflects the character and peace of Christ Himself. No circumstance, no sin, no personal failure, no person, no disappointment, no limitation, and no other such thing can separate a child of God from the love of God or thwart the Author of Faith from continuing His work of conforming believers into the image of Himself (*Romans 8:29, 35*). The path that leads to true joy is found by actively cooperating with, not rebelling against the circumstances that will ultimately work together for one's own good and God's own glory. Peter understood the human difficulty of trusting what God says in His Word rather than his own emotions or reasoning. He also recognized a person's need to detach himself from what he wants and trust instead in the work and love of Christ. He comforted suffering believers by saying, "Wherefore let them that suffer according to the will of God commit the keeping of their souls to him in well doing, as unto a faithful Creator" (*1 Peter 4:19*). In other words, a Christian needs to turn his focus from the temporal pleasure he has lost to the eternal joy he will gain and rest in the love of God!

Throughout the Psalms, David reveals the anguish of his soul when being persecuted unjustly, when he sinned and brought loss upon himself, when he lost the loyalty of dear friends, when loved ones died, when his baby son died, when children rebelled in terrible ways, when he was sick, and when he experienced many other trials of various kinds. Yet David consistently turned his attention from his loss and his disappointment and looked instead to God for help and mercy. As a result, he learned to trust and praise God in all these situations and discovered the help and healing properties of hope in Christ. He was able to confidently declare, "The Lord also will be a refuge for the oppressed, a refuge in times of trouble" (*Psalm 9:9*). "I had fainted, unless I had believed to see the goodness of the Lord in the land of the living" (*Psalm 27:13*). "The Lord is my strength and my shield, my heart trusted in Him, and I am helped; therefore my heart greatly rejoiceth; and with my song will I praise him" (*Psalm 28:7*).

In a nutshell, when a believer persists in a state of sorrow that is not accompanied by hope and confidence in the promises and presence of God, he is engaging in a pernicious combination of the sins of self-pity and unbelief, which can ultimately lead to a paralysis of responsible thought and action. This kind of reactive depression, or sorrow without hope, is more than a normal reaction to life problems—it is a symptom of wrong views of God, one's self, and God's purpose for one's life. Most importantly, this sorrow without hope often reflects an unwillingness to let go of emotional attachments that one has to people and things that relate to this world and emotionally attach one's self instead to Christ Himself.

DEPRESSION
AS A
REACTION
TO
Personal Failure

CHAPTER FOUR

One's perception of personal failure has an extremely powerful effect on how he will react when he experiences the effects of his human frailties and failures. Failure experienced in any significant area of life contributes to the despair and lethargy commonly associated with depression. What a person believes, and the significance he attaches to each perceived failure, will determine the way he responds to the failure.

In an ideal world, mankind would never fail. Humans would never use poor judgment, never embarrass themselves with inappropriate behavior or unwise decisions, and never cave in to fear of any kind. Every endeavor would culminate in breathtaking success and every "should" would be replaced with a "could." Humans would be everything they ought to be and do everything they ought to do. In short, they would be perfect, even as God is perfect. Man understands that perfection isn't possible in this life, and he knows he is constrained by human limitaitations. Yet he sometimes lives as though perfection is possible simply because he wishes it were. This causes him to react to failures by excusing them, denying them, covering them up, rationalizing them, or agonizing over them. When a person reacts in this way, he invariably begins to experience depression and increased irritability. His reactions reveal the depth of importance he places on an unrealistic standard of perfection as well as his despair at being unable to attain it. A more humble and realistic approach is to acknowledge failure, accept limitations, and simply confess sin when sin is a factor. A Christian needs to consciously do his best to grow in grace, but at the same time, he must recognize basic human frailties and refuse to agonize over them.

To be sure, God is perfecting His children and conforming them to be like Himself. God works in people in ways they cannot do themselves; for no human being, by his own willpower and strength, has ever yet attained Godlike character completely untainted by sinful selfishness or pride. Though man highly esteems character and aspires to be known by virtuous qualities, he falls miserably short of his own ideal. Throughout history, human virtue and the corresponding perils of human vice have been core topics woven throughout classic literature, art, religion, and philosophy. The triumph of good over evil and the battles waged in the process glorify man and dominate the most common themes in popular forms of entertainment even today. Human beings *want* to identify with the heroes of their stories and if it were possible, be supernaturally endowed. The desire to be righteous is good if it leads a person in humility to the foot of the cross where he can receive God's mercy and grace. The same desire is devastating if it lifts a person up in pride and causes him to imagine he can be righteous in and of himself apart from the work of God.

The most beautiful and powerful angel in heaven became discontent with the limitations God placed on him and determined in his heart that he would rise to be *like* God (*Isaiah 14:12-15*). His pride destroyed him, but it didn't stop him from enticing Eve with the same lust that consumed his own heart—the promise of supernatural power. "Eat it," he urged her, "for God doth know that in the day ye eat thereof, then your eyes shall be opened, and ye shall be as gods, knowing good and evil" (*Genesis 3:5*). Eve desired something she saw as a virtue—but she desired it on her own terms, apart from God's mandate. Perhaps she wondered how wanting wisdom or knowledge could be wrong. The desire for wisdom is not wrong, any more than the desire to be like Christ is wrong. Wisdom, however, is not found instantaneously on man's terms. It must be received through God's terms in obedience to Him. Wisdom begins with the fear of the Lord—something Eve lacked at the moment she yielded to Satan's suggestion and put her trust in him rather than God.

Trying to acquire God's wisdom through man's methods is arrogant and evil. Since the fear of the Lord is to "hate evil, pride, and arrogancy," such a prideful error only takes man further from wisdom, not closer to it (*Proverbs 8:13*). Likewise, the fruit of the Spirit (Christlike character) is not acquired by human means, through hard work, or determination. The Spirit's fruit is the by-product of one's relationship and fellowship with Christ (*Galatians 5:16-17*). Perfect virtue, which includes the quality of joy and peace, is not something a person receives in one day, though he would certainly love it to be so. Rather, Christlike character is something that one becomes day by day as he grows in grace and engages in battle against the foes that are yet a part of his daily life. No man has ever enjoyed the victory of battles won without enlisting in God's army and taking up arms to fight against the foes of fleshly desires, worldly enticements, and Satan himself. The victory is certain, for God promises it to be so; but it is not won on man's terms. Christians must fight with God's implements, on God's terms, in God's way. Paul reminds Christians that the weapons of a spiritual warfare are not of this world (*2 Corinthians 10:14*). They are mighty through God, and capable of pulling down strongholds that enable the enemy to defeat Christians. And where are these strongholds? They are in the mind. Therefore, believers are instructed to bring "into captivity every thought to the obedience of Christ" (*2 Corinthians 10:5*).

All of God's children have been commissioned to do battle with an enemy that is without *and* within. There is no such thing as instant victory apart from spiritual boot camp, knowledge of Christ, and experience. God's way is to work in people and through people, often in spite of people's frailties, in His way and in His time. We are transformed to be like Christ by the use of many means, and over the course of a lifetime we learn to walk with God in humility and dependence on Him through every trial—including the trials of personal failure. Obedience and faith are learned only as we exercise daily obedience and faith. Though Christians may be anxious to be perfect and free from the weakness of humanity, God is not in any hurry to free His children from the limitations He has so purposefully and wisely placed upon them. Failure, to be sure, is a tool in God's hand just as surely as it is a tool in the hand of a wise parent who is patiently training his child. For instance, it is good, not bad, that a child mismanages an allowance and learns the consequences of wanting instant gratification. Such a failure builds the framework of experience that has the potential to teach him principles of managing money before he mismanages a credit card or a paycheck as a grown man. Consider how often Peter failed, yet the Lord Jesus patiently worked to guide and teach him throughout his ministry on earth. Peter learned as much by his failures as he did by his successes.

Peter did not instantaneously learn how to trust the Lord or how to bring every thought into obedience to Christ. It was not through lack of desire or enthusiasm. Peter had both. Yet the Lord did not demand Peter have the abilities of an adult believer when he was yet a baby believer. Rather, Christ understood the process of growth and moved Peter ever closer toward maturity, using every failure as a rung in the ladder that helped him in an upward climb toward dependence on Christ. Peter's immaturity and self-sufficiency come to light in his comments to the Lord when the disciples had gathered together with Him in the upper room...

The Lord met with His disciples to have a last meal with them, to give parting instructions before His crucifixion, and to pray and fellowship with them. The gathering begins with the Passover meal, which is followed by Christ pouring water into a basin and washing the disciples' feet as an illustration of their calling to serve one another in love and humility. When the Lord comes to Peter, Peter immediately objects to the gesture of love, imagining that his own desire to wash the Lord's feet instead was a more righteous act. Christ does not harshly condemn

Peter, but firmly admonishes him until he willingly complies. A little while later, the Lord began to explain to the men what was about to take place and how He was about to leave them. Again Peter objects, confidently asserting his intention to follow the Lord even if it means death. Clearly, Peter was confident at this moment that his own determination and love for Christ were sufficiently strong enough to carry out such a loyal and brave act. Imagine his surprise when the Lord answered him with these penetrating words, "Will thou lay down thy life for my sake? Verily, verily, I say unto thee, the cock shall not crow, till thou hast denied me thrice" (*John 13:38*).

Peter most likely sat very quietly as the Lord Jesus continued speaking to the disciples. Jesus concluded by lifting His eyes toward heaven and praying for them as well as for other believers. The Scriptures do not reveal what Peter or the others were thinking as the Lord prayed, but one can imagine they were touched with wonder as they pondered His gracious words. He spoke of their obedience and love of His Word. He prayed they would be transformed by His truth, that they would be filled with His joy, and that they would be made perfect (complete and mature) in unity with Himself and the Father. Finally our Lord concludes with the anticipation of one day being all together with Him in heaven, perfectly complete, and enveloped in His love (*John 17*). Jesus ends His prayer, knowing every request to the Father would be granted, and yet knowing the process of maturing was not yet complete. Peter would learn to react to personal failure correctly only by experiencing the sorrow of reacting incorrectly.

Jesus had foretold to Peter that Satan desired to have him in order to sift him like wheat, and that He had prayed for Peter, that his faith would not fail (*Luke 22:30-31*). Jesus knew Peter's human efforts would fail. His prayer was that when (not if) he failed, his faith would not fail. Peter *needed* to fail in order to grow in faith and become useful in God's service. Christ wasn't at all perturbed as He spoke, but strangely enough, simply urged Peter to strengthen his brethren after he repented. Certainly one would think Peter would be silenced into submission after hearing this, considering it was spokendirectly by the one Peter recognized as the Messiah, the Son of God. Yet only a few hours later, Peter was again asserting his own determination by whacking off the ear of Malchus, the slave of the high priest, with his sword as Jesus was about to be led away from the garden of Gethsemane (*Luke 22:50; John 18:10*). Again, Jesus responds with mercy and patience by healing the ear that was cut off by impetuous Peter.

As Jesus had predicted, all the disciples fled and distanced themselves from Him after the soldiers took him away. Peter managed to watch from a distance as Jesus was led to the high priest's house. He quietly intermingled with others who were warming themselves by a fire in the courtyard, hoping he would not be recognized. To his dismay, he was confronted by three different people, and vehemently denied knowing Christ each time. The Scriptures say, "And immediately, while he yet spake, the cock crew. And the Lord turned, and looked upon Peter. And Peter remembered the word of the Lord, how he had said unto him, Before the cock crow, thou shalt deny me thrice. And Peter went out, and wept bitterly" (*Luke 22:60-61*). Peter responded to his failure much as others do who desire to please God, yet know they have miserably failed Him. He wept bitterly. Peter's heart was filled with sorrow, not just for what was taking place with Jesus, but because he knew his determination and resolve had melted in the face of sinful self-preservation. He was faced with the cold reality that he was not only capable of sinning against the God He loved, but had done so without hesitation to the point of angrily cursing at those who confronted him.

The Bible does not say where Peter fled to after his betrayal. Only John, Mary the mother of Jesus, and two other women appear to have stayed nearby throughout the crucifixion. Eventually, Peter had to have been told what happened and, no doubt, his despair was all the more bitter knowing what he had done. The next mention of Peter is very intriguing. After Jesus had risen from the dead and three women had seen an angel who told them Christ was alive, they were told to tell his disciples, *and Peter*, that they would soon see him (*Mark 16:7*). The Lord in His compassion for Peter knew he would need that extra assurance of His love. It is highly possible Peter was experiencing the sorrows of depression in all its darkness and hopeless despair. Yet with Christ, there was no rejection and no condemnation—only love and continued efforts to bring Peter to a place of spiritual understanding. Peter, in response, ran to the sepulcher and saw for himself the empty tomb. The Scriptures tell us he "wondered in himself at that which had come to pass" (*Luke 24:12*). He had a glimmer of hope, though the lesson was not complete nor his fears yet dispelled.

Shortly after the news of Christ's resurrection, the disciples, including Peter, did see and hear Jesus for themselves on two separate occasions. Still Peter's heart was not at peace, nor his guilt resolved. A few days later, Peter made a decision to go fishing and invited other disciples to join him. Peter's attention turned back to fishing, perhaps because he no longer thought himself worthy to be a disciple, or perhaps simply because he didn't know what else to do. When a night of fishing ended without a catch and morning saw them coming to shore without anything to show for their efforts, they caught a glimpse of someone on the beach, cooking fish over a fire. In a manner so like Jesus, He calls out, "Children, have ye any meat?" Perhaps Christ was smiling a little when the men answered no. Then as He had done when they had first met three years before, He told them where to cast their net for fish. Just as before, the nets were filled and immediately the men knew it was Jesus. The goodness of God so moved the heart of Peter that he immediately put on his clothes and swam to shore ahead of the others. There they found breakfast sizzling on the fire and heard the Savior invite them to dine.

What must Peter have been thinking while they all sat together enjoying that specially prepared meal? Certainly, he was not interested in making bold declarations at the moment, nor was he the first to speak. After eating, Jesus turns to Peter, knowing exactly what was in his heart and what needed to be changed. He doesn't accuse Peter, condemn Peter, or in any way speak harshly to him. Instead Jesus asks a simple question that penetrated right to the problem that troubled Peter. "Simon, son of Jonas, lovest thou me more than these?" (*John 21:15*). Jesus purposely addressed Peter by name, and specifically asks if Peter loves Him. Jesus is teaching Peter how to react appropriately to failure and how to appropriate His grace and forgiveness. The issue isn't whether or not Peter loves Christ, but whether Peter loves Christ more than anything else,

41

with all his heart. Three times Peter responds with an affirmation of his love, just as he had denied Christ three times. Christ's response was very simple and brings the message he had spoken before the crucifixion to remembrance. Before the crucifixion Christ says, "This is my commandment, that ye love one another, as I have loved you" (*John 15:12*). After His resurrection, He asks Peter directly to demonstrate his love by serving others, feeding His lambs and sheep (*John 21:16-17*).

The next time Peter is mentioned is after Christ's ascension into heaven. Peter and others gather in an upper room for prayer, and Peter is leading the group and preaching the Word of God boldly on the day of Pentecost. Peter's focus was no longer on his past failure; his focus was on Christ's forgiveness and Christ's love and righteousness. Peter did not suddenly become perfect. What changed was his reaction to failure and his understanding of Christ's love and power. After Peter and John healed a lame man in the temple and caused quite a stir among the people who saw what had happened, Peter spoke to the people and said, "Why look ye so earnestly on us, as though by our own power or holiness we had made this man to walk? And his name through faith in his name hath made this man strong, whom ye see and know: yea, the faith which is by him hath given him this perfect soundness in the presence of you all" (*Acts 3:12,16*). Peter was finally beginning to understand that a believer's strength and power are only in Christ and His righteousness and His power. All attention and all glory are to God, not to those He imputes righteousness to or uses in His work. God receives the preeminence.

Christians do not bring glory to God when they wallow in the disappointment of their failures. They bring glory to God when, by faith, they gladly receive His gracious promises to forgive the moment they humble themselves to admit their sin and weakness. Failures are a part of life. They are inevitable. They have the capacity to drive people to Christ in humility and repentance, or drive them further into themselves until they and their problems are all that matter to them. When believers see failures as God sees them and recognize how He uses them, believers are freed from self-condemnation and all the chains of defeat that go along with that ugly mind set. Seeing failure as Christ sees failure means they will believe by faith what He has said. "There is therefore now no condemnation to them which are in Christ Jesus" (*Romans 8:1a*). When we ruminate on our disappointment, embarrassment, shame, and weakness, we become morose and unbelieving in our ever-consuming self-pity. Trying harder will not bring victory. Reciting self-determination mantras are useless. Righteousness and spiritual wholeness will not be produced but by repentance and faith in His name.

Repentance toward Christ is the door through which the joys of God's love and mercy are bestowed upon His children. Christians shouldn't react to failure by running from the painfulness of facing their failures honestly. Instead, they should bow at the feet of a loving God and tell Him what He already knows. God is not demanding perfection. He is, however, leading His dear children to face the truth and causing them to know that He *is* demanding humility. David learned this same life lesson. In his prayer of confession recorded in *Psalm 51* he says, "Behold, thou desirest truth in the inward parts; and in the hidden part thou shalt make me to know wisdom" (verse 6). Further into the prayer he repeats, "For thou desirest not sacrifice; else would I give it; thou delightest not in burnt offering. The sacrifices of God are a broken spirit; a broken and a contrite [humble/repentant] heart, O God, thou wilt not despise" (verses 16-17). Sometimes the only means of healing a fatal disease is through painful surgery. Though it hurts, the end result is freedom from pain and suffering, and then finally, joy in submitting to the process. David had experienced this wonderful phenomenon as well after pouring his heart out to God in complete confession and repentance. He is able to pray with confidence, "Restore unto me the joy of thy salvation; and uphold me with thy free spirit" (verse 12).

DEPRESSION
AS A
REACTION
TO
The Failure of Others

CHAPTER FIVE

5

Learning to face and deal with failures in a spiritually constructive way is a difficult process for every believer. As one grows in grace, he learns to see through the eyes of faith in order to be truthful about himself, yet at the same time recognizing "there is therefore, no condemnation," for Christ took all the punishment and condemnation for sin when He died in man's place at Calvary. What a joy to discover that He deals with those who are His children with love and mercy, correcting them in patience, without anger or disgust! A more difficult lesson, perhaps, is learned when believers must face the failures of others in a way that is pleasing to Christ. The failures of others aren't normally life-shattering, unless those failures in some way hurt or affect another person directly. It is then that a person feels the downward pull of his human emotions and is tempted to center his thoughts and concerns on the injustices and sins that have been committed against him or those he loves.

How would a person respond if he were asked to show kindness toward people who were known to be cruel and ferocious, intolerant toward religion of any kind, and hateful enemies of his race? We further hear that these brutal people have wreaked havoc in this person's own city, killing and raping members of his own family in bloodthirsty, sadistic ways? Would anyone relish the idea of traveling to this country to share with these cruel people the love and mercy of God? Most people would ask God Himself to wipe them off the face of the earth. Such was the attitude of Jonah, a man who was asked by God to go to the city of Nineveh to preach and warn wicked people of God's judgment on their sin. Can anyone really blame Jonah for wanting to run the other direction? But run he did, boarding a boat headed in the opposite direction of Nineveh in an effort to escape the wishes of the Lord.

Jonah soon learned that no one is able to outrun God or escape from His gaze or the discipline of His hand. In the midst of a storm God Himself created, Jonah was thrown overboard and swallowed by a great fish that the Lord Himself had prepared for this purpose. From within that dark prison in the fish, Jonah prayed until his will was broken, and he was ready to yield himself without reservation to God's purposes. It is of no surprise that Jonah was ready to obey the Lord's instructions to go to Nineveh and preach the message of the Lord *after* the fish expelled him on dry land.

Immediately upon entering the city, Jonah began to preach that God would destroy Nineveh in forty days. As much as Jonah had not wanted to step foot in this wicked city, he did not seem to mind telling these people that God's judgment was about to fall. After all, they deserved to be punished. To Jonah's astonishment, the people of the city believed God and repented of their sins, from the least important right up to the king who sat on the throne. The king went so far as to proclaim a fast and instructed the people to "cry mightily unto God; yea, let them turn every one from his evil way, and from the violence that is in their hands" (*Jonah 3:8*). This was not a revival Jonah wanted any part of. In fact, the Scriptures say Jonah was very angry when this happened. He did not share God's willingness to show mercy, nor did he like the fact that God was not showering fire and brimstone upon them for their evil cruelties.

God's plan was not Jonah's plan, nor did it satisfy Jonah's desire for vengeance or his outrage against the evil that had been committed against his own people. It made no sense to Jonah and seemed unjust. In anger and disgust, Jonah prays that God would take his own life from him because he believed he would rather die than live in such an unhappy state of mind. Interestingly, God ignores the request for death and instead asks Jonah a simple question that goes right to the heart of the matter. "Doest thou well to be angry?" (*Jonah 4:4*).

The fact that these people had done wicked things was not in question. Nor was it in dispute that they had victimized innocent people unjustly. Seldom do people of today encounter cruelties of the nature Jonah faced, yet people of all ages suffer as victims of sinful acts of others at some time or another simply because people live in a world that is filled with violence and sin against God. For the unbeliever, such painful atrocities have no purpose or plan. They are simply senseless acts of selfish violence or hatred that are inflicted without cause. The believer, on the other hand, is protected from evil that has no purpose or eternal value. When Christians do suffer, God promises that He sees and hears the cries of His children; and He "is the avenger of all such" people (*1 Thessalonians 4:6*). The Lord has warned believers that in this life they will suffer; but in eternity, there will be no evildoers, and there will be no more victims of sinful or selfish acts. While believers live on earth, however, they will be the recipients of the offenses of others. Christ warns, "It is impossible but that offenses will come; but woe unto him, through whom they come!" (*Luke 17:1*).

The human response to injustice is quite typically one of anger. A person's mind is focused on the wrong that has been done to him, its unjust nature, and the pain it has caused. Wrong may have been done; it may indeed have been unjust; and it may have caused much pain; but eyes of faith are required to see beyond the reality of grief and look at the bigger picture rather than the pain of the moment. First, we do not know or understand how injustice could ever accomplish anything good. God does not cause people to sin, yet God is able to use even the sins of man to accomplish His eternal purposes. This is something we cannot possibly comprehend, because man's ways are not God's ways. Yet God is infinitely more wise and loving and just than we could ever imagine, and He accomplishes righteousness in ways that perplex and amaze us. Nebuchadnezzar stated, "...that the living may know that the most High ruleth in the kingdom of men, and giveth it to whomsoever he will, and setteth up over it the basest of men" (*Daniel 4:17*). In man's utopia world, ungodly men would not be rulers or leaders. Yet in the world God oversees, He is able to use even the vilest men to accomplish His purpose.

Joseph, who was unjustly sold into slavery by his own brothers, unjustly accused by Potiphar's wife and thrown into prison, then unjustly forgotten though he had extended a favor toward another who could have helped him could have easily become bitter and lost all confidence in the plan of God for his life. For years God appeared distant and unmerciful. Yet Joseph accepts what happens without question and continues to serve and love God even in prison. When at last God orchestrates the events that would catapult him to great honor and prestige as a leader in Egypt, Joseph continues to exalt God and serve Him. Then later, when his brothers are brought by God to Egypt and brought to repentance for their sin against their brother, Joseph tells them, "But as for you, ye thought evil against me; but God meant it unto good, to bring to pass this day, to save much people alive" (*Genesis 50:20*). Christians do not always see the plan of God, nor understand how it is working for their benefit and His glory. Christians only have God's promise that it is.

Sometimes we live to see God's plan plainly revealed. Other times, the sins of others are not made manifest until they stand at the judgment of Christ after death. This delay should not distress us. Paul reminds young Timothy, "Some men's sins are open beforehand, going before to judgment; and some men they follow after. Likewise also the good works of some are manifest beforehand; and they that are otherwise cannot be hid" (*1 Timothy 5:24*). Paul encourages believers who are perplexed by confusing difficulties not to draw quick conclusions. He says, "Therefore judge nothing before the time, until the Lord come, who both will bring to light the hidden things of darkness, and will make manifest the counsels of the hearts; and then shall every man have praise of God" (*1 Corinthians 4:5*). Humans are not God, therefore they do not have the ability or right to execute vengeance or recompense evil that is done to them. Paul compassionately pleads with those who are wronged unjustly, "Dearly beloved, avenge not yourselves, but rather give place unto wrath; for it is written, vengeance is mine; I will repay, saith the Lord" (*Romans 12:19-21*). The words "I will" are an affirmative promise. God *does* deal with the sins of the unrepentant, yet He does not always deal with them in the ways or the time frame that a hurting person desires.

Sometimes, God does not execute judgment immediately because He is giving the offender space of time to repent. At other times He withholds immediate retribution because there is a purpose that the offense will accomplish in time. Because people cannot know or understand the mind of God in these matters, they are commanded to simply trust Him and rest confidently in the assurance that He loves them and will make all things work together for their good and His glory (*Romans 8:28-29*). This trust can be difficult, but Christians can be comforted, knowing God is able to turn around for good that which others or Satan meant for evil. Peter wrote, "Yet if any man suffer as a Christian, let him not be ashamed; but let him glorify God on this behalf... wherefore let them that suffer according to the will of God commit the keeping of their souls to him in well doing, as unto a faithful Creator" (*1 Peter 4:19*).

Not only is injustice that is committed against others ultimately dealt with, it is also able to accomplish a purpose, and make possible an eternal reward if we will put our trust in God. Jesus tells us, "Blessed are *ye, when* men shall revile you, and persecute you, and shall say all manner of evil against you falsely, for my sake. Rejoice, and be exceeding glad; for great is your reward in heaven; for so persecuted they the prophets which were before you" (*Matthew 5:10-12*). In times of sorrow and oppression that is inflicted by others, the believer has a refuge to flee to, for God promises, "The Lord also will be a refuge for the oppressed, a refuge in times of trouble. And they that know thy name will put their trust in thee; for thou, Lord, hast not forsaken them that seek thee" (*Psalms 9:9-10*). A believer's comfort, then, is in the promises of a God who is trustworthy and full of love for His own. Anger does not comfort. Attempting to understand cruel offenses does not comfort. Comfort comes when we believe and anticipate God's ultimate justice and over ruling power in our lives.

It is not always an easy thing to observe others who seem to be "getting away with murder" live what appears to be a happy or blessed life. What we see on the outside, however, is not always reality. Asaph, like many Christians today, was anxious to see God crush his enemies. He had a hard time understanding why it appeared those who loved God were suffering while those who were arrogant and defiant against God were not. *Psalm 73* is a description of such pondering that begins with Asaph being discouraged by what he sees and ends when he sits in the presence of God and begins to see the larger picture. He says, "Behold, these are the ungodly who prosper in the world; they increase in riches…When I thought to know this, it was too painful for me; until I went into the sanctuary of God; then understood I their end." When Asaph focused on what appeared to be injustice, he was overwhelmed and discouraged. However, when he looked at the situation from an eternal perspective, from beginning to end, he came to a completely different conclusion that resulted in completely different emotions. Christians today can receive the same comfort when they examine situations in the context of eternity.

The Psalm ends with Asaph concluding that it is good for him to draw near to God and put his trust in the Lord so that he could declare all His ways. In *Psalm 119:71*, David comes to this same conclusion and declares, "It is good for me that I have been afflicted; that I might learn thy statutes." In *Psalm 119:67-88*, David describes the lies, the hypocrisy, the pride, and the persecutions committed against him by wicked people. Yet at the very same time, he asserts his trust in God and his esteem for the Word of God that gives him understanding and hope in the midst of such mistreatment. It spite of his grief, he refocuses on God's promises and is encouraged and uplifted by his confidence in God's Word. As one reads this Psalm he can see the delicate balance between faith and truth and the struggles being fought in David's mind. He could have sulked and pouted, just as Jonah did, but David chose a different path that had a far different outcome.

Whatever happened to Jonah after the great revival in Ninevah? The Bible says he planted himself on a hill overlooking the city and waited, hoping God would destroy this repentant population on day forty. The sun was hot and Jonah was miserable, both physically and emotionally. The Lord caused a gourd to grow over Jonah, providing him with shade and relief from the sun. The next day, however, God caused a little worm to destroy the gourd so that it withered and died. Adding to the situation, He caused a miserable, sandy, and hot wind to blow on Jonah so that together with the heat of the sun, Jonah became exceedingly uncomfortable. Predictably, Jonah complained and being angry and depressed, again wishes he were dead. He tells God, "It is better for me to die than to live" (*Jonah 4:8*).

God isn't at all moved to join in Jonah's sentiments, but asks, "Doest thou well to be angry for the gourd?" (Jonah 4:9). The Lord has provided a living object lesson to help Jonah understand the foolishness of his despair and the lack of mercy in his heart. Yet in his immaturity and self-pity Jonah childishly retorts, "I do well to be angry, even unto death." Jonah doesn't get it, so God replies, "Thou hast had pity on the gourd, for the which thou hast not laboured, neither madest it grow, which came up in a night, and perished in a night. And should not I spare Nineveh that great city, wherein are more than sixscore thousand persons that cannot discern between their right hand and their left hand; and also much cattle?" (*Jonah 4:11*).

God wants Jonah to stop and consider what it is he is so upset about. Jonah has forgotten that he himself has been forgiven for sins and has been the recipient of God's love and mercy. Only days earlier God answered his pleas for mercy and miraculously delivered him from being eaten by a fish. He sees only the injustice done to him by others, not the grace God extended to him. Jonah is so obsessed with his desire for vengeance and his displeasure over what has taken place that he has no pity for the many children in Nineveh who would have been destroyed had their parents not come to repentance. Jonah has pity for a plant that has no soul and does not live forever, yet none for human beings that will live forever in a literal heaven or a literal hell.

When Christians react with anger or despair over the failures and hurt-ful acts of others, they are much like Jonah, focusing on temporary pain rather than the eternal destiny of souls for whom Christ died. We want mercy and grace for ourselves, but we do not always want it for others. We wrongly believe we deserve God's love, while our enemies do not. We want to decide who is worthy to be forgiven and who is not, who should be punished and who should be spared. In our pride and igno-rance, we put ourselves unwittingly in the place of God and attempt to make decisions only God can make. It is not enough for us to know God is just and does deal with the wicked and does balance the books exactly right in the end. We want justice and we want it now, immediately. This thinking is not only foolish; it is totally incapable of moving the heart of God to respond as we wish.

All the anger and sorrow, crying and pleading will not make God ca-pitulate to our childish demands. Our responsibility is to revere God as God, trusting Him to work as only He can, committing ourselves into His care, knowing that in Him we have comfort and hope for the future. His way is always far superior to our way. No one "gets away" with anything. God *does* deal with those who refuse to repent—but not in the way we wish or at the time we want it done.

Suffice it to say, we must quietly rest in the love and comfort of our Sav-ior, knowing He alone is just and wise enough to handle every offense. "Wherefore doth the wicked contemn God? he hath said in his heart, thou wilt not require it. Thou hast seen it; for thou beholdest mischief and spite, to requite it with thy hand; the poor comitteth himself unto thee; thou art the helper of the fatherless" (*Psalm 10:13-14*). To ignore this truth is to persist in a rebelliousand immature state of mind. It is like the response of a two year old who throws himself on the floor, kicking and screaming because his mother will not buy him the candy he wants so badly. It's not always easy for a child to trust the judgment of a mother, but he is certainly happier and more content than the child who angrily reacts with tantrums when he doesn't get his own way.

Jonah does *not* do well to be angry. He, like so many other believers who are depressed and angry, forsakes his own mercy by refusing to forgive. This error presumes there are some who do not deserve God's mercy while others (such as one's self) do. The fact is, *not one* of us deserves God's grace or mercy for the Lord has said, "There is none righteous [just/worthy], no not one. There is none that understandeth, there is none that seeketh after God" (*Romans 3:10-11*). He who is unforgiving imagines he has merited his own righteousness and is who he is by his own strength and wisdom. In essence, he puts himself in a different category of guilt than others and fails to remember that it is only by God's grace and work in a life that one is able to respond to truth and learn to hate sin and love God. Forgiving does not minimize sin or the wrong done to one's self or others, nor does it demand one to trust an offender or remove the judicial consequences of the offense. Rather, it recognizes the two parts of forgiveness and is willing to completely entrust all offenses to the only One who is qualified to judge and exact vengeance. This forgiveness is unconditional and emulates God's willingness to forgive on the basis of Christ's redeeming work on the cross. On the other hand, granting forgiveness, which is different than forgiving from one's heart, is given only when a person repents of his sin, and makes reconciliation, restoring the fellowship that was broken by the sin possible. (See *Secrets of a Happy Heart*, chapter 4.)

Those who imagine they cannot forgive, in reality, *will not* forgive and will not trust God for appropriate justice in His time and His way. Sadly, these are often in no less danger than those who refuse to repent. The story told by Christ in *Matthew 18:23-35* ends with a warning to any who will not forgive the offenses of others. Christ tells His listeners that God will deliver to the tormentors those who will not, from their heart, forgive every man his trespasses. Certainly,the tormentors of depression imprison the spirit of all who arrogantly presume they, but not others, deserve God's mercy and forgiveness. The only key that will unlock the doors of this chamber of terrors is the key of forgiveness. "For if ye forgive men their trespasses, your Heavenly Father will also forgive you: but if ye forgive not men their trespasses, neither will your Father forgive your trespasses" (*Matthew 6:14-15*).

DEPRESSION
AS A
REACTION
TO
Self-Indulgence

CHAPTER SIX

6

Self-indulgence comes in so many forms it would be difficult to identify and define them all. Certainly, enjoying one's self is not the problem. God gives us richly all things to enjoy (*1 Timothy 6:17b*). The problem is that man does not naturally deny himself or govern his desires well. Man's natural tendency is to avoid discomfort while gravitating toward whatever pleases him. This tendency turns the ability to enjoy God's blessings into things that have the potential to rule and enslave man when they are not controlled. If we are not able to control our appetites; our appetites are then able to control us. Good things, such as food, entertainment, leisure time, sleep, work, money, sex, or hobbies become things that rule us when misused or indulged in excess. At the same time, those things we naturally want to avoid, when indulged excessively, render us increasingly more aversive toward fulfilling responsibilities and completing tasks that are distasteful, but necessary.

Once this double-edged sword of self-indulgence gets a stronghold in our lives, we begin to discover its incredibly destructive nature. The more we are enslaved to our desires and the more we avoid distasteful responsibilities or unchangeable events, the more we will suffer the effects of depression and irritability. When the pursuit of happiness rather than the pursuit of godliness becomes a major focus in our life, we tend to make choices on the basis of what makes us feel happy at the moment, not on what ultimately brings joy in the long run. Suddenly, the effects of overindulgence, such as large credit card bills or a sink full of dishes, loom over us and seem far more overwhelming than they are simply because it is our own fault they have become such a problem. Instead of repenting of the indulgence that caused the situation and rectifying the problem, we continue in the same avoiding behaviors, perpetuating cycles of irresponsibility and despair. That God is interested in our happiness is not in question. The Bible is filled with references that give insight into what produces joy and happiness and encourages Christians to enjoy God's blessings. Where Christians run into difficulty is at the point when their method and God's method of producing joy differ!

We insist we will be happy when life is easier and our desires are met, while God simply isn't in agreement with our shortsighted human perspective. His way recognizes the importance and relationship between what takes place today and what will take place in our life for eternity. He will never lead His children to forfeit tomorrow's rewards and joy for today's comfort. Our dear Savior knows that when we reach heaven's shores we would look back and regret having our own way. So He, in wisdom and love, allows His children to experience even pain and sorrow if doing so will produce that which insures long-term happiness. Christians are faced with the daily choice to ignore God's warning and indulge their human desires wrongly, or deny their human reasoning and desires in order to learn a moment-by-moment walk with God. Knowing when a normal enjoyment of God's blessings crosses over into enjoying God's blessing to the exclusion of God's commandments is a function of spiritual maturity and wisdom. One thing is certain—sinful indulgence always leads to future sorrow and loss, while denying self the temporary pleasure or relief to do God's will always lead to future joy and gain. In the following passage, Christ purposely moves from the problem Christians have with indulgence to the desires they have as human beings and then to the perspective of eternity.

"Then said Jesus unto his disciples, If any man will come after me, let him deny himself, and take up his cross, and follow me. For whosoever will save his life shall lose it; and whosoever will·lose his life for my sake shall find it. For what is a man profited, if he shall gain the whole world, and lose his own soul? Or what shall a man give in exchange for his soul? For the Son of man shall come in the glory of his Father with his angels; and then he shall reward every man according to his works" (*Matthew 16:24-27*).

The Scriptures are filled with exhortations to keep our focus on the eternal benefits of serving and trusting Him in whatever situation we are going through today. In the same context, we are warned of the eternal loss we will experience as a result of choices we make to indulge ourselves wrongly today. To take up one's cross means to willingly submit to the death of a self-ruled life. To deny one's self means a person must first have unshakable faith in the promises and character of God, because Christians cannot now see eternity or the rewards of self-denial that Christ talks about in the Bible. We walk through this life by faith, not by sight, knowing one day we will see clearly and then be exceedingly glad that we put our trust in God's ways rather than our own human reasoning. But for now, we cannot even imagine the things God has for those who love Him above themselves. We only know that the pain and disappointment we experience for a moment in this life cannot be compared to the joy and rewards we will have by trusting God now.

Hanging on to the scraps of pleasure found in our human desires prevents us from recognizing the true pleasures and riches that are found only in denying self and living instead to please God. Clinging to our own ideas of happiness is as foolish as stubbornly keeping a tight fist wrapped around a handful of pennies rather than letting the coins drop to the ground so we can reach for a check worth a million dollars. Preserving our self-life rather than losing it for Christ's sake is a short-sighted choice far more foolish than this. Yet we Christians routinely make little choices in daily life that, in essence, reflect what we want, the pennies or the check. A four year old who is given the choice of immediately receiving a handful of coins or waiting a week and receiving five handfuls, typically chooses the immediate gratification of the handful. A three year old that is asked to give up his favorite toy in exchange for a check worth ten times as much refuses to relinquish the toy for a piece of paper that means nothing to him. The problem of self-indulgence is similar in that it is essentially a problem of shortsightedness and spiritual immaturity. It sacrifices future lasting joy for temporary immediate gratification and then suffers the effects of depression that are a built-in result.

The words of Paul the apostle who understood this human struggle well is prevalent to Christians today: "...For our light affliction, which is but for a moment, worketh for us a far more exceeding and eternal weight of glory; while we look not at the things which are seen, but at the things which are not seen; for the things which are seen are temporal; but the things which are not seen are eternal" (*2 Corinthians 4:8-11,17-18*).

The temptation to grab the delights of temporary immediate gratification at the expense of future lasting joy is presented to Christians daily. A believer might put off fulfilling the duties of his respective work responsibilities in order to watch a television program, spend money that should be used to pay a debt, oversleep instead of rising early enough to start the day with prayer, socialize too long rather than going to bed at a reasonable hour, or consume alcohol or drugs in order to escape the discomfort of facing problems. None of these "little" daily indulgences seems to have eternal significance any more than how one reacts to life's afflictions seems to have a corresponding eternal effect. Yet they do. Little indulgences soon add up to big consequences. Not only are we made in such a way that the accumulation of little acts of irresponsibility produce depression, they also lead to a future loss of eternal joys. Little indulgences that become a habit can lead to a harmful indulgence when it really does matter. Christians must learn to see with eyes of faith that which cannot be seen by the human eye in order to wisely choose to endure a present difficulty or fulfill a distasteful responsibility rather than grab for instant gratification or escape.

Perhaps no indulgence is so enslaving as indulging the mind and allowing it to think and dwell on whatever it pleases. Many who live a disciplined life outwardly live an extremely undisciplined life inwardly. The undisciplined mind is allowed to wander and ruminate on whatever displeases and whatever is desired. Sometimes large amounts of time are spent mentally sorting through and reviewing what has happened or what one wants to happen to the extent that such thinking interrupts the ability to concentrate, work, or sleep. Dwelling on problems or wrongs committed against us makes acceptance, forgiveness, or reconciliation impossible. It paralyzes us emotionally and spiritually to the point where we do not address or resolve problems the way God would have us do, but rather, we become increasingly more consumed and embittered about our problems. Before long, bitterness becomes a way of life until we are hardened and blinded by it. Harboring grudges, refusing to forgive, dwelling on our disappointments, or refusing to deal with problems eventually leads to a tormented mind, riddled with the effects of depression. Worse, it ignites physical problems and robs us of the joy simply resting in Christ's love and management of our lives brings. Indulging in destructive thinking is a habit that is tenacious and deceptive, for Christians typically deceive themselves into believing such thinking is reasonable, necessary, helpful, or comforting. Nothing could be further from the truth. It is a habit as enslaving as drug use and every bit as destructive.

We become whatever we think about and dwell upon (*Proverbs 23:7*). If a believer dwells on wrongs done against him, he becomes bitter and defensive. If a believer thinks about himself constantly, he becomes selfish and self-centered. If a believer focuses his attention on what is wrong with something or someone rather than what is good, he becomes critical and heavyhearted. If a believer fantasizes about things he wants, he eventually becomes obsessed with obtaining them and unhappy with what he has. If a believer's thoughts constantly gravitate to past failures, he becomes defeated and discouraged. If he dwell on fears, or the things that *could* happen, he becomes fearful and anxious. If he thinks about the magnitude of his problems and his insufficiency to solve them, he becomes weary and overwhelmed. When we think about something long enough, we will be consumed by it and changed by it. Ever so slowly, in tiny incremental steps, we become what we think about until at long last, it envelops our personality and becomes our character even while we deny it is so. "For as he thinketh in his heart," the Bible states, "so is he" (*Proverbs 23:7*). What we think about, what we believe, and what we desire has the power to produce either joy or sorrow. One cannot indulge in sinful thought patterns without experiencing the devastation and depression that follows in its wake. Thankfully, just as surely, one cannot remain depressed when thoughts, beliefs, and desires are brought into harmony with God.

The antidote to thinking wrongly is to deliberately choose to think rightly, for one cannot think right and wrong at the same time. Sinful and undisciplined thinking crushes and destroys all remnants of the peace Jesus has promised to those who keep their thoughts focused on Him. With comforting relevance to today, the Bible says God "will keep him in perfect peace, whose mind is stayed on thee; because he trusteth in thee" (Isaiah 26:3). The command to "Be careful [anxious] for nothing; but in every thing by prayer and supplication with thanksgiving let your requests be made known unto God" is followed by a promise, "And the peace of God, which passeth all understanding, shall keep your hearts and minds through Christ Jesus" (*Philippians 4:6-7*). Paul concludes this statement to the Philippian believers by telling them to *deliberately choose* what they think about. "Finally, brethren, whatsoever things are true, whatsoever things are honest, whatsoever things are just, whatsoever things are pure, whatsoever things are lovely, whatsoever things are of good report; if there be any virtue, and if there be any praise, think on these things" (verse 8). There is no room in this list for sexually impure thoughts, hateful thoughts, covetous thoughts, or any number of sinfully indulgent thoughts that a man, woman, or child might engage in.

It is no coincidence that the Scriptures speak of peace so often in relation to our thought life and relationship with Christ. We are told that "to be carnally minded *is* death; but to be spiritually minded is life and peace" (*Romans 8:6*). To be carnally minded means that one's thoughts and desires are centered on satisfying one's self to the extent that everyday life is lived apart from any consideration of God or God's Word. What is most important to a carnally minded person is what pertains to *me* because satisfying *me* is believed to be the source of happiness. Rather than producing happiness, such a quest produces a pernicious form of self-centeredness that destroys real joy and leads to despair. It is like drinking salt water to quench one's thirst only to discover it makes one thirstier than ever.

To be spiritually minded is just the opposite. The spiritually minded person orients his life around a relationship with Christ and His Word. His greatest delight is forgetting himself altogether and sharing the joy he has in his relationship with Christ with others. He's happiest serving the needs of others rather than satisfying himself. We often picture a spiritual person as one who does and does not do a list of forbidden things, who attends church and uses a lot of spiritual jargon in conversation. As the Pharasees of old, we like to imagine that a disciplined life or good works commend us to God and automatically make us "spiritual." Christ taught something far different. He repudiated those who would follow the letter of the law and ignore the fact that God wants our hearts, not our efforts to do what we believe to be good things. It's not about what we do or do not do, but about who we love, who we know, what our minds are fixed upon, and who we are inside. We can do all the right things and look quite spiritual without ever giving our hearts to Christ. But we cannot give our heart to the Lord Jesus Christ and fall in love with Him and not want to please Him, rather than ourself.

Paul the apostle found grace and peace, not in fulfilling the law as a Pharisee and gaining the esteem of those who would honor and admire him, but in a relationship with the Lord Jesus Christ that cost him his pride and denied him temporary earthly pleasures he once lived for. From his heart he could write to young believers, "Grace *be* to you and peace from God the Father, and *from* our Lord Jesus Christ…" (*Galatians 1:3*). Even while suffering in a Roman dungeon, Paul's heart was filled with the love and peace of God. In a situation where Paul could have justifiably been depressed, he was instead joyful. This was not the result of human will power. It was the supernatural result of Paul's relationship with Christ and his deliberate choice to be content with God's provision for himself and instead focus on the spiritual needs of others. Paul's mind was focused on those things that bring lasting peace and joy to others, not on temporary pleasures for himself or on temporary hardships either(*Philippians 4:8-9*).

We are no match against our propensity to indulge our sinful human desires if we ignore the warnings and urgings of Christ to live in fellowship with Him, delighting to know and obey His Word. In fact, Paul tells us that our human bent toward sinful self-indulgence engages in war against the Holy Spirit who indwells every believer and gives a desire to do what is right and pleasing to God. A believer's hope and power for overcoming lies in his union with Christ and in a decision to walk *with* Him, rather than *away* from Him. Paul says, "This I say then, walk in the Spirit, and ye shall not fulfil the lust [selfish desire] of the flesh. For the flesh lusteth [wars] against the Spirit, and the Spirit against the flesh; and these are contrary the one to the other; so that ye cannot do the things that ye would" (*Galatians 5:16-17*).

Indulging the flesh when it screams to be satisfied in sinful ways only satisfies for a moment. Soon afterward, the bitter taste of guilt and the painful consequences of sin land us in a pit of sorrow and despair. Over and over throughout the Scriptures God warns that our own sinful self-indulgence and refusal to deny our flesh brings great sorrow and regret. Sin *is* pleasurable; otherwise it would not be the trap that it is. Its pleasure, however, lasts only long enough to entice and ensnare us, and then it turns ugly. Solomon warned his sons, "Bread of deceit is sweet to a man; but afterwards his mouth shall be filled with gravel" (*Proverbs 20:17*). Consider any method in which the flesh seeks unrestricted satisfaction or seeks to avoid life's necessary hardships and then take a long hard look at where such indulgence leads. It's never a pretty picture, whether it be self-pity, refusals to resolve disputes, laziness, sleep, food, drugs, alcohol, gossip, bitterness, endless soap operas, adultery, neglect of family, pornography, anger, or a thought life out of control. Sinful self-indulgence in these and hundreds of other forms always appeals to our selfish desires and always destroys our joy, and if we are truly saved, always brings guilt, followed by depression if we fail to repent. Ultimately, it can destroy our life as well as the lives of our children and family.

Jeremiah preached to people who catered to their own desires and then blamed God for the misery that their own ways brought upon them. He tries unsuccessfully to reason with them in an effort to lead them to the restored peace and joy of repentance toward God. He asks them, "Hast thou not procured this unto thyself, in that thou hast forsaken the Lord thy God, when he led thee by the way? Thine own wickedness shall correct thee, and thy backsliding shall reprove thee; know therefore and see that it is an evil thing and bitter, that thou hast forsaken the Lord thy God, and that my fear is not in thee, saith the Lord God of hosts. Your iniquities have turned away these things, and your sins have withholden good things from you" (*Jeremiah 2:17,19;5:25*).

Apart from repentance toward God (a change of mind and direction), guilt leaves a path of misery and destruction that has inevitable consequences in the inward life of believers and unbelievers alike. Even the most ungodly psychologist recognizes and acknowledges the devastating effects guilt has on the human mind and body. God did not make us in such a way that we are able to cope with the mental torment of sinful self-indulgence and the guilt it inevitably produces. Rather, sorrow and guilt act as warning lights that flash to get our attention so we will repent and correct the problem before it causes untold loss in our lives. If the oil light in your car flashes to warn that the engine is out of oil and dangerously hot, you would not destroy the light or ignore it. Rather, you would be grateful for the warning and immediately deal with the problem before your engine was destroyed.

The presence of guilt is an indication something is wrong spiritually just as the presence of pain is an indication something is wrong physically. All our efforts to manage guilt our own way, or escape from its grip by our own means, will ultimately fail. Ignoring sin, attempting to drown it out with various distractions, rationalizing sin, blaming others for our sinful choices, punishing ourselves for our sin, or justifying our sin only leads to more misery and mental torment. There is no peace to those who reject God's gracious means of dealing with life's problems in a right way. Peace eludes those who scoff at the idea that repentance is the only means by which we can find the joys of forgiveness.

Isaiah the prophet contrasts the misery of sin with the joy of God's forgiveness by testifying, "Behold, for peace I had great bitterness: but thou hast in love to my soul *delivered it* from the pit of corruption: for thou hast cast all my sins behind thy back" (*Isaiah 38:17*). David understood the connection between peace and a right relationship with Christ as well. He tells us, "Great peace have they which love thy law and nothing shall offend them" (Psalm 119:165); and "Blessed [how happy] is he whose transgression is forgiven, whose sin is covered" (Psalm 32:1). David describes the anguish of his soul when he refused to repent and wallowed in his grief and despair. Then he describes his relief and joy when he comes to his senses and acknowledges his sins and confesses them to God (*verses 3-7*). Indulging our secret passions seems so inconsequential while we are momentarily escaping life's difficulties by enjoying its pleasures. At the last, however, it is an insidious deception that has the power to blind, entrap, and enslave even the strongest Christian.

DEPRESSION
AS A
REACTION
TO

Despair

CHAPTER SEVEN

7

Ahithophel was King David's trusted advisor for many years, so it seems quite odd that he would defect from David's long standing circle of friends to join Absalom's murderous revolt against his father. It is even more puzzling to read that Ahithophel put his household in order and killed himself when his advice to immediately attack David's entourage before David has time to organize was overturned by Hushai's advice to wait. What would prompt such a devastating act by one who is known for wisdom and discernment? It makes little sense—unless you also know that Ahithophel was Bathsheba's grandfather. No doubt Ahithophel's proximity within David's court gave him an insider account of David's adulterous relationship with his married granddaughter. He knew of David's attempts to cover his sin and was undoubtedly aware that he had in some way misused his authority to cause Uriah's untimely death. Ahithophel was powerless to bring David to justice or to change the course of events that made Bathsheba David's new wife. He was, however, able to spend a great deal of time dwelling on the horror and selfish arrogance of a king who would do such a wicked thing. Adultery, murder, and hypocrisy are not qualities that endear a leader to those who serve him—even less so when it affects family members you love. Can you imagine Ahithophel's indignation and disgust to think that this king he had served so faithfully and loyally for so many years would betray his trust and bring such sorrow and harm to his family? There is no written account of Ahithophel confronting David regarding his sin. Ahithophel's anger and bitterness boiled silently in his heart for several years until he found an outlet for his hatred by joining Absalom's rebellion against the king.

The Scriptures indicate that Absalom was well aware of Ahithophel's secret hatred for David and called for him when his conspiracy against the king was underway. Ahithophel had found someone else who was disgruntled and bitter, and no doubt, the two fed each other's indignation for David and worked together to unify the people against the king and orchestrate his overthrow. It must have given Ahithophel a sense of delight to see David driven from the city and to anticipate his capture by Absalom's gathering army. Already, Absalom had followed his advice to rape the concubines of David in a tent set up on the palace rooftop for that purpose. Ahithophel moved with deliberate precision and began to carry out a well-laid plan to exact judgment against David. He was determined to hurt David, as he believed David had hurt him. His plan was to first humiliate David, and then kill him with his own sword. He left only one thing out of his equation—God.

David, meanwhile, expressed surprise when a servant told him that Ahithophel was among the conspirators advising with Absalom. All the years of secret hatred and bitterness that Ahithophel felt toward David was being revealed in the heat of a revengeful war. The stage was set. Ahithophel took his position with an angry young man and relied on personal cleverness and reasoning to destroy David. Meanwhile, David took his position with the outcasts of Israel and relied on the mercy and intervention of God. "Oh God, I pray thee, turn the counsel of Ahithophel into foolishness," he prayed (*2 Samuel 15:31*).

One could hardly blame Ahithophel for being upset with David, given the circumstances. However, Ahithophel reacted to David's sin in ways that were sinful. Ahithophel's calculated actions did not bring any relief to his troubled heart whatsoever; they did not change David's heart; nor did they help lead David to repent of his sin. Ahithophel's actions certainly did nothing to comfort Bathsheba or other family members who looked to him for leadership. Ahithophel's response was centered on his own feelings and his own sense of loss and indignation. He failed to see or believe that God was actively working behind the scenes in David's life, holding David accountable for his sin and dealing appropriately with him. Evidently Ahithophel didn't believe God could be trusted to deal with David's sin justly, and grew impatient when he didn't see sufficient immediate retribution. In his mind, Ahithophel must have believed David was "getting away" with too much.

In the process of time, Ahithophel was able to justify his betrayal of David and his involvement in Absalom's conspiracy. As far as he was concerned, David was the guilty party who deserved what he got, while he was the innocent victim who had a "right" to avenge his family's honor. Anger had poisoned Ahithophel's heart to the point where he was blinded by the shortsightedness of his vengeful solution. He felt righteous, turning against a man he viewed as a hypocritical, manipulative murderer. Yet, ironically, by taking matters into his own hands, he himself became a hypocritical, manipulative murderer.

Ahithophel was bent on destroying David, yet he had enough understanding of God to recognize that the overturning of his advice by Hushai was an indication the Lord was intervening on David's behalf. He understood that Absalom, by accepting Hushai's advice, was sealing his fate. He intuitively knew his short reign would soon end in defeat. At that moment, all of Ahithophel's plans were shattered. Bitterness filled his heart, but there would be no satisfying it with revenge on David. Athithophel realized he was not going to get his way. He was so bitter and so filled with determination to succeed in his plans that he was devastated when things didn't go as he had hoped. All that mattered to him at that moment were his revengeful plans, and those plans were crushed completely.

What followed was not a cry for help—it was the expression of an angry man who was so consumed with himself and his own grief that he could not see the utter foolishness and error of his response toward David's sin. Rather than dealing righteously with his understandable grief over David's wicked actions years earlier and confronting David, Ahithophel refused to handle the matter in a God- honoring way. He demonstrated a lack of regard for God's sovereign rule over David and God's right to judge and deal with David's sin as He determined best. By attempting to exact revenge on David, Ahithophel unwittingly put himself in the place of God, usurping God's authority. Ahithophel had become arrogant and foolish just as David was when he sinned with Bathsheba and plotted Uriah's death. Both made plans believing they could have their own way and, at the same time, thwart God's judgment.

Ahithophel became so controlled by his own emotions that he focused intently on finding a way to exact revenge. He had no room left in his heart to consider God's love and wisdom in the matter, let alone God's plan for his own life. He did not take into consideration God's promises to him and to his family, for he saw only the pain of the moment, not the way God ultimately vindicates the innocent and blesses those who trust Him. Ahithophel could not trust God and wait, or rather, he *would* not. He was so consumed with himself and his despair that he proceeded to commit a tremendously selfish act—he murdered himself. Destroying *any* life is an act of murder because life does not belong to man; life belongs to God who gave it. To be precise, destroying one's own life is self-murder. Ahithophel's choice to murder himself brought temporary grief to his family, to Bathsheba, and to David; but it did not stop life from going on. His torment did not end with death as he had hoped. Rather, his torment simply extended into eternity with no further opportunity to repent or have a different ending written regarding his life. God did not forsake Ahithophel. Rather, Ahithophel forsook God. Had Ahithophel chosen to put his trust in God rather than destroy his own life, he would have lived to see his great grandson become Israel's most wise and prosperous king. He would have seen David's repentance and observed the terrible consequences David paid for his sin against his family, the nation, and God Himself. Ahithophel deceived himself into believing all hope was gone, and death was his only escape from the torments of his embittered mind. Yet somewhere in eternity, Ahithophel is living today, still regretting his last act of defiance that he can never undo. He sees clearly by sight what he chose not to see by faith back then. The distress and despair that seemed so overwhelming doesn't look that way from the perspective he now has in eternity.

While there are numerous lessons we could extract from the lives and choices of these men, perhaps the most obvious is simply this: It is in the quiet recesses of the heart that our destiny is determined, for out of it come the choices we make that will ultimately result in joy or sorrow. We will act consistent with what we believe and what we desire, particularly as it pertains to what we believe and desire concerning the things of the Lord. Ahithophel trusted in his own heart and as a result, came to believe there was no hope or purpose for him to live. David, on the other hand, trusted in the Word of God and as a result, believed in God's mercy and ability to turn around even the most impossible of circumstances. Athithophel looked inward. David looked upward.

When things were at their worst and David was as low as low could be, he often complained and became overwhelmed as a result. As soon as he turned his attention from himself and his problems to the faithfulness and mercy of God, his spirits were lifted and his outlook changed. Many of the Psalms begin with David expressing the dark and gloomy thoughts of a man consumed in sorrow only to end with the hope and joy of a man expectantly looking to God for deliverance. *Psalm 142* begins with David telling us, "I cried unto the Lord with my voice…I poured out my complaint before him; I shewed before him my trouble." Then David goes on to lament that no matter where he looked, "there was no man that would know me; refuge failed me; no man cared for my soul." David is saying, in essence, "no one understands me and no one really cares about my soul." Sound familiar? Whereas some have stayed permanently in this pit of despair, David turns to God and cries for help. Then he asserts his confidence in God his refuge and declares his belief that God will ultimately deal bountifully with him for His own name's sake.

Again in Psalm 77 we see the psalmist crying to God, refusing to be comforted, complaining about his misery and the fact that his spirit is overwhelmed with sorrow. In fact, he is so distraught that he says he can't sleep or speak. Then he begins talking to himself and reasoning, not with the perspective of defeat, but with the perspective of hope as he remembers the mercy, promises, and power of God. The more he recalls to mind the wonderful works and love of God, the more his thoughts take on a whole different tone. The momentum builds until the psalmist is filled with joy and confidence and ends on the highest note of praise. In every incidence where David finds himself in despair, he recalls the great character and promises of God and reaffirms that he believes what God has said is true.

David was not a sinless man. Certainly he was no less a sinner than Ahithophel. The difference between the two men is that David humbled himself before God and put his trust in God's mercy. He appealed, not to his own righteousness, but to the righteousness, mercy and loving-kindness of God. God delighted in David, and comforted him, *because David believed in Him*. We get a glimpse of David's heart as we listen to him pray, "Be thou my strong habitation whereunto I may continually resort…Deliver me, O my God, out of the hand of the wicked, out of the hand of the unrighteous and cruel man. For thou art my hope, O lord God; thou art my trust from my youth" (Psalm 71:4-5).

Contrast this attitude with the attitude of one who trusts, not in God or God's Word, but in his own heart and ability to reason. Time after time God demonstrates the foolishness of trusting one's heart and leaning on one's own understanding, for invariably it leads to tragic endings as senseless and unnecessary as Ahithophel's. Acts of suicide—self murder—are the expression of one who trusts his own heart over the promises of God. No person's situation, problem, sin, or failure is hopeless, for God's grace is equal to any need and His promises are available to all who will call upon Him and put their hope and trust in His mercy. Had

Ahithophel turned to God in repentance and put his trust in Him, he would have found God faithful as promised and would have found the very same mercy and forgiveness that David found.

DEPRESSION'S

Antidote

CHAPTER EIGHT

8

Distress, despair, forsaken, destroyed—these are words that describe the darkened thoughts and emotions of depression. There is no hope in these words, no anticipation of God's good and gracious character, no trust in the reality of God's sovereign work, and no confidence in God's love and interest. Left to fester in a mind that is inwardly focused, distress and despair wrongly convince a soul he is forsaken by God and destroyed. The truth is, we who are God's redeemed are never forsaken and never destroyed by God. "We are troubled on every side, yet not distressed; we are perplexed, but not in despair; persecuted, but not forsaken; cast down, but not destroyed" (*2 Corinthians 4:8-9*).

Paul said these words to encourage Christians who were suffering for the cause of Christ. He made no attempt to minimize the severity of their trials. Rather, he acknowledged their difficulties and sought instead to strengthen their faith while undergoing them. He wanted them to know that the Christian never suffers in vain, never suffers in vain, never suffers forever, and never suffers without a purpose or reward. He testified in the fourth chapter of *2 Corinthians* that a life given whole-heartedly to serve Christ and become more like Him was a life worth living. His "secret" to withstanding adversity with grace and confidence wasn't really a secret. "We faint not," he said, because we have received mercy from God, because we serve Christ rather than ourselves, be-cause we believe what Christ has promised, because we believe the Gos-pel is the hope of the world, and because we look forward to spending eternity happily rejoicing in all of God's work.

Paul was not suffering for his own sake, but gladly suffering for the sake of others so they could experience the love and glory of God as he did. He concluded by saying, "but though our outward man perish, yet the inward man is renewed day by day" (*2 Corinthians 4:16*). What happened outwardly did not determine Paul's joy or sorrow. What determines his strength and happiness in any situation depended on what took place inwardly, in his heart, as he fellowshiped with Christ and drew strength from truth found in His Word on a daily basis. He would have fainted and grown discouraged just as any other human being would—had he not kept his focus firmly fixed on his purpose for living and on the faith-fulness of Christ Himself. David recognized this same truth and states, "I had fainted [given up hope], unless I had believed to see the goodness of the Lord in the land of the living [in this life here on earth]. Wait on the Lord; be of good courage, and he shall strengthen thy heart; wait, I say, on the Lord" (*Psalm 27:13-14*).

Thus far we have spent the greatest part of this study discussing a va-riety of ways depression can be fueled by our reaction to life's trials and difficulties. This is by no means an exhaustive list. However, it is hopefully sufficient to encourage readers to consider not only these, but other ways in which reactions to major disappointments or difficult situations produce despair and hopelessness rather than joy and hope in the midst of a storm. Many may be reacting wrongly to boredom, lone-liness, spiritual confusion, difficult marriage problems, a life-altering illness, problems with a job or family, financial problems, or problems that make daily life difficult or oppressive; and the result is discourage-ment or depression. Whatever the difficulty, God promises all who will believe Him that He has available sufficient grace and help to not only cope with problems, but cope with them in a spirit of confidence and joy. The only thing hindering such a seemingly impossible transformation of our spirit is our own unbelief. God invites all of us, with no exceptions, to "taste and see that the Lord is good, for blessed [happy] is the man that trusts in him" (*Psalm 34:8*).

When great storms arise (as they inevitably will), we have two choices in the way we approach Christ. We can be like the apostles who came to Jesus gripped with doubts and fear when the storm became fierce saying, "Master, carest thou not that we perish?" Like them, we might also be tempted to ask Jesus, who cares enough about us to know how many hairs are on our heads, and cares enough about us to die on the cross in our place, "Lord, don't you care?" Or, we can choose to be like Paul who confidently sought the Lord when he was caught in a tempest that put his ship and all aboard in great peril. When all hope for survival was gone, Paul encouraged the sailors "to be of good cheer" because he had been assured by God that their lives would be spared if they would follow his directions. Paul testified that an angel, sent by the God whom he belonged to, stood by him in the night and comforted him (*Acts 27:23*). Paul chose to come confidently and boldly to the throne of God's grace in order to obtain the mercy and grace to help in a time of need (*Hebrews 4:16*). God invites *every* believer to do the same. He promises *all* who belong to Him that the angel of the Lord encamps around those who fear Him, and delivers them (*Psalm 34:7*).

When we cry to God for help, we must be ready to do what He tells us to do. God has specific instructions that will resolve our despair *after* we step out in faith and *obey* Him. Sometimes we become passively paralyzed in our fear and despair, and then wonder why God does not miraculously dispel the storm and lift us out of our pit of sorrow. We might be tempted to complain and justify our hopelessness because "we already tried that." We may have cried to God in our trouble, but if we did not also do whatever God instructs us to do in our particular trouble, then we did not "already try that." The Bible promises that God is faithful and dependable—He *cannot* lie. He knows the kinds of trials and sorrows we might face in this world and will not allow us to experience more of them than we are able to bear. When we *do* face life's trials, God promises He will always provide a way to escape, so that we can endure it. "There hath no temptation [trial/trouble] taken you but such as is common to man [others have endured what you are going through successfully and so can you!]; but God is faithful [He can be trusted because He cannot lie], who will not suffer [allow] you to be tempted [tried] above that ye are able; but will with the temptation [trouble] also make a way to escape, that ye may be able to bear it" (*1 Corinthians 10:12-13*).

Loosening Depression's Grip

Perhaps many are tempted to stay curled up in bed with the covers pulled over their head because they do not feel like getting up or fulfilling the responsibilities God has given them to do. Many may feel as though there is no hope, or that their broken heart or crying to God has not been heard. Quite possibly many have earnestly prayed, as countless others like them have, that God would miraculously take the black cloud of depression away and restore their joy. Many feel forsaken when they awaken each morning just as miserable as ever, as though God has ignored them or is unconcerned about their difficulty. Perhaps many have convinced themselves that God is cruel because He has not instantaneously dispelled their misery or removed their trial as they have begged Him to do.

Dear believer, God wants His children to experience His joy more than even His children want to experience it. He longs for His own to take those first steps of faith to *move* in the direction He wants them to go. He does have an answer, a way of escape, prepared just for those who are experiencing difficulty. A depressed person may be seeing a big brick wall in front of him—but by looking a little closer, one will see there is *always* a little door somewhere in that brick wall that will allow a person to keep going until that day when the sun will come out in all its brightness until it dispels every gloomy black cloud. No one ever finds that way of escape who throws himself on the ground in despair and weeps in bitter agony, refusing to get up and go forward. There are no exceptions, my friend. As much as God loves His own and promises to help them, He will not capitulate to a person's demands no matter how loudly or brokenheartedly a person cries. God has promised that He will not withhold any good thing from His children who walk uprightly (*Psalm 84:11*). He *will* hear and deliver us out of *all* our troubles—but we must deliberately make the choice to put one foot in front of the other and do what God wants us to do, no matter how we might feel.

A believer needs to go to God's throne of grace. They need to settle any matter they know to be sinful. "Lay aside every weight, and the sin which doth so easily beset us, and let us run with patience the race that is set before us, looking unto Jesus the author and finisher of our faith; who for the joy that was set before him endured the cross…" (*Hebrews 12:1-2*). A believer needs to ask for mercy and grace to help in time of need. Then a child of God should ask what he knows to be the right thing to do *today*, right *now*. Then he must set out to do it, even while he proceeds to investigate and seek for every possible way of escape that God has or will provide in his trial. A person struggling with depression should decide to deal with problems, seeking for possible solutions, *after* he has put in a good day of work and fulfilled whatever responsibilities God has given him to do for the day. By setting aside a particular time each day to work on problems, a person does not allow himself to stop living in order to dwell on how he feels or on his problems. As a result, a person is not allowing even good sorrow and grief to cause him to neglect responsibility. Rather, he needs to seek God's strength to continue doing what he needs to do, even in spite of a heavy heart. He just keeps on doing what is right, even though he may not yet be experiencing an improvement in the melancholy mood he is battling. "For you have need of patience, that, after you have done the will of God, you might receive the promise" (*Hebrews 10:36*).

Is this the Lord's day? Then believers should be at church to assemble with other believers as God has directed them to do. By looking for ways to serve others, a person uses the gifts God has given him to be a blessing to His people. Doing what God has directed can be done in a number of ways: by praying for those who are yet lost in their sins, by worshipping the God who saved him and keeps him by His power, by singing praises to God, by giving a portion of his income to the Lord, by listening to the Word of God as it is preached, and by asking God to open his eyes so he can see wonderful things out of His law. Many will say, "But I don't feel like it." Why, of course, a person who is depressed won't feel like it. Being consumed with feelings of depression leaves a person feeling emotionally drained, tired, unsociable, and gloomy. It would be most unusual if a depressed person did *feel* like it. So he should do it anyway, because following feelings is not the means God provides as a person's way of escape.

If one has just experienced a tremendous loss, he might naturally prefer to be alone; and it is hard to look forward to the future or resume the routines and demands of living. However, following one's feelings will only keep him in the pit of despair. A person needs to accept how he feels, but ignore it at the moment. Instead, he moves forward, asking God to encourage, doing what is right to do, putting troubles aside, and turning his attention, his eyes, upon Jesus. The words of this beloved song written by a saint who once felt the same way encourages those who hurt: "O soul, are you weary and troubled? No light in the darkness you see? There's light for a look at the Savior, and life more abundant and free! Turn your eyes upon Jesus, look full in His wonderful face; and the things of earth will grow strangely dim, in the light of His glory and grace."

Is it Monday, and time to report to work? Then a person should be there on time, ready to fulfill his responsibilities in a way that will glorify Christ. "Whatsoever thy hand findeth to do, do it with thy might…" (*Ecclesiastes 9:10*). Some say they have trouble concentrating. Of course, a depressed person would. That is one of the physiological effects that occur when a person's mind has been sorrowing and focused inwardly for a long period of time. The way to get the mind redirected is to focus it outwardly on particular responsibilities no matter what they are, even though a person will not feel like it. By keeping thoughts and minds channeled constructively all day long, little by little people are able to concentrate as they once did before. Work is honorable. It is a blessing and a means to serve God. God has given mankind six days to do work and has made people in such a way that they cannot be happy or content if they neglect to labor for their sustenance. Of course, pressing the snooze button ten more times or calling in sick—seems appealing. But God says that mankind *needs* to work, and will be happiest if people put in a good day of labor whether we like it or not, whether they feel like it now or not. When tempted to avoid hard work, a person should consider the words of *Hebrews 12:2-3*. "Looking unto Jesus the author and finisher of our faith; who for the joy that was set before him endured the cross, despising the shame, and is set down at the right hand of the throne of God. For consider him that endured such contradiction [rebellion] of sinners against himself, lest ye be wearied and faint in your minds."

God warns people not to love sleep, "lest thou come to poverty; open thine eyes, and thou shalt be satisfied with bread" (*Proverbs 20:13*). Christians need to ask themselves if they are avoiding unpleasant responsibilities to fulfill ones that are more agreeable? A Christian should do the unpleasant ones first, knowing that God is pleased when His children humble themselves in this way, and gives grace to the humble. "Humble yourselves therefore under the mighty hand of God, that he may exalt you in due time; casting all your cares upon Him; for he careth for you" (*1 Peter 5:5-6*). Every occupation, no matter how seemingly glamorous, has its share of tedious details that must be attended to.

A Christian, struggling with depression or not, should serve his employer to the very best of his ability. Homemakers need to attend to the home and its affairs with everything they've got. Are there little children to care for? Then one needs to give one's self wholeheartedly to care properly for these little heirs to eternal life that God has placed in one's care. Many may be retired or ill. Then they also need to use their time to serve God in ways that maybe they could not before. Teaching the younger generation is a great calling. We all need to be zealous to work, no matter what kind of work is done, whether paid or not, whether it is little or much; for God has many promises to those who are diligent and dependable in their work, who refuse to give in to the human tendency to be slothful. "Seest thou a man diligent in his business? he shall stand before kings; he shall not stand before mean men" (*Proverbs 22:29*).

Is this Saturday, a time to set aside work and be refreshed? A person should make plans to enjoy family, cultivate friendships, and pursue hobbies and talents, which are gifts from the Lord. God has said that He sets the lonely in families so they can enjoy and strengthen one another. "God setteth the solitary [lonely] in families; he bringeth out those which are bound with chains; but the rebellious dwell in a dry land" (*Psalm 68:6*). If one does not have immediate family members, God has still given him a church family. Cultivating friendships in one's church family is refreshing, just as it refreshed Paul throughout his busy, and trying, missionary life. Paul made friends by being a good friend and by ministering unselfishly to others in their need. He mentions by name people who are not always well known to us, who were a tremendous blessing to him. Men such as Stephanas, Fortunatus, Achaicus, Titus, Onesiphorus, and friends in Sidon refreshed his spirit with their love and friendship.

Is this a day in which there is discretionary time to plan enjoyable activity and enjoy the beautiful world in which we live? We should not neglect to do so—deliberately—knowing God has lovingly provided even this for our benefit. When the children of Israel entered the Promised Land and finished conquering it, the Scriptures tell us that God gave them rest and intended for them to enjoy the beauty of the land that He had given to them (*Joshua 1:16*). Using a portion of our earnings for enjoyment is also a gift of God, according to *Ecclesiastes 3:13*. "And also that every man should eat and drink, and enjoy the good of all his labour, it is the gift of God." People who do not cultivate interests and hobbies for personal enjoyment are far more likely to experience debilitating depression in response to trials and difficulties. We need to experience this important part of our life and make the decision to discover by trial and error interests that we will be able to pursue for the purpose of relaxation, fellowship, and enjoyment.

One may say he has no pleasure in anything right now. This is quite normal when we have been enduring a long season of sorrow in which our minds have been consumed with painful thoughts. Such a person will need to get out in the fresh air and deliberately make himself see the beauty that lies all around him. He can take time off from work and trials just to look at nature and marvel at God's handiwork. A person should begin small, by reading a funny book, calling a lighthearted friend, taking a walk in the woods, walking along a lake, watching a sunset, or playing a game with his children. He can find something he might like to learn about, pick up that instrument he used to play, ride the bike he used to ride, or finish the project stored away. Better yet, a person can find someone who also enjoys relaxing activities. By having a companion, a struggling person has to go out even though he does not feel like it; but somewhere down the road, he will begin to notice the spark returning and his smile coming back. Whatever load someone must carry will be a lot lighter if he will treat times of refreshment as something necessary and blessed by God.

What does God want us to do *today*? Right now. We should concentrate on this alone. God walks with us through a trial one step at a time. We don't often know exactly what steps we need to take or how the problem will gradually unfold. What we must do is learn how to take one day and one problem at a time without stretching our necks to see what is at the end of a very winding road. We can only see one bend at a time, so it is futile to waste any effort wondering what lies several miles of bends ahead. We can be comforted that God gives us what we need to know to take the next step and respond today. Then as we round that corner, He prepares us to face the next. He doesn't give us our monthly bread—He gives us our daily bread. He doesn't give us tomorrow's grace, for tomorrow isn't here. He gives us today's grace, because today's grace is what we need. Jesus told us not to worry about tomorrow, because tomorrow will have enough challenges of its own. He knows that the trials we face in one day are enough to handle. We must focus, then, on one step at a time. "Take therefore no thought for the morrow; for the morrow shall take thought for the things of itself. Sufficient unto the day is the evil thereof" (*Matthew 6:34*).

Joy Comes in the Morning

David came to the end of his life filled with grateful praise for all of God's blessings. He had tasted both the joys and sorrows of human experience, but most importantly, the joys and sorrows of his Christian experience. God records David's highs and lows, his success and his failures, times of great blessing, and times of great turmoil during which God disciplined and corrected him. Throughout the Psalms we read David's most intimate and heartfelt emotional expressions of both joy and sorrow throughout every phase of his life. Now as an old man who is ready to join other saints in heaven, he testifies that God is indeed faithful, merciful, and good. In the thirtieth Psalm, David assures those who will travel the same way he came, that although God may allow a short time of suffering for a specific purpose, He always removes the darkness of night just as quickly as His dear child turns to Him with a contrite heart and trusts Him. Verse five says, "...in his favor is life; weeping may endure for a night, but joy cometh in the morning."

WHY AM I
SO
Depressed

PART TWO

INTRODUCTION TO THE APPLICATIONS

It is our prayer that you have been encouraged by reading this book and are beginning to see the morning rays of sunshine peeking from behind those dark clouds of depression. The following section of this book is included to further strengthen your understanding and help you come to the place where you can be thoroughly filled with joy and be able to confidently sing praises to God for all He has taught and brought you through. When Israel was distressed and wallowing in the turmoil of trouble, the Bible tells us, "Then they cry unto the Lord in their trouble, and he saveth them out of their distresses. He sent his word, and healed them, and delivered them from their destructions" (*Psalm 107:19-20*). God still hears when His children find themselves swallowed up in trouble and cry to Him for help. And He still heals the same way that He healed Israel when they cried to Him. He sends His Word, and heals them. It is for this reason that we are providing readers with several biblical application studies and a constructive method to systematically deal with the torments of depression.

In order to make your Bible study most profitable, a three-ring notebook with several sheets of paper to use as a journal to write personal answers and discoveries is suggested.

As you work your way through each application, you may be surprised to find that God provides many practical solutions that you may not have thought of once you begin to understand where, how, and why the depression began. Once you have read the following overview of this suggested approach, you will want to begin working on the biblical application lessons, one at a time.

As you prayerfully work through the remainder of this book with your pen and Bible in hand, you will discover many Bible truths that have the power to dramatically change the way you think and react. Pray as David did, "Open thou mine eyes, that I may behold wondrous things out of thy law" (*Psalm 119:18*). Remember that even little changes are capable of producing big results. If you will earnestly seek God's truth and learn to trust Him over subjective feelings, you will discover as others before you, that obeying God's truth does set you free from all that would take away the joy God has for His children. Understanding and applying God's truth, as opposed to knowing His truth, will result in a joy and contentment that truly does pass all understanding—even your own.

Before going on…

Stop!

Don't keep walking until you take the time to stop and look ahead to where you are going! Remember that God has a divine order that is not understood by those who do not know Christ or rely on His Word. He tells us who are His own that He will do what we cannot when we simply do what He has given us the ability to do. We naturally want our physical, earthly needs met; and God does not ignore such needs and desires. However, He instructs us to *first* seek what is important to Him, and to desire His righteousness, to be like Him. Then, He promises, He will see that all our heart's longings are met abundantly. We tend to want God to meet our needs and desires first, and then believe we will respond by pouring our energies into seeking what pertains to Him. This order will never work, for it puts God in second place instead of making Him our number one priority. He must always be first in our heart and life, and then we can confidently expect Him to work in ways we could not even have imagined. "Seek ye first the kingdom of God and His righteousness, and all these things shall be added unto you" (*Matthew 6:33*).

Rather than making relief your main objective, put your energy instead into seeing this problem in the way God wants you to see it and allowing it to draw you closer to Him. Make discovering what He wants you to learn through this experience your greatest objective. Once you have your heart set in the right direction for the right reasons, then proceed by identifying when, how, and what your depression is, concentrating on potential underlying problems rather than things that are more apparent on the surface. Relief will naturally come once you begin understanding and applying God's truth to your situation. On a separate sheet of paper in a notebook, write your answers to the following questions:

When did your depression begin? How has it developed? Has depression been a problem for several years or in other instances when you have been faced with a difficult trial or experienced a significant loss? If applicable, how did the depression subside in the past, or how did you resolve it? What do you believe you could be reacting to at present? Are there several problems, one major problem, or one major problem and several others that are related to it? Can you list the thing or things you have lost that are related to this depression? Why are these things important to you, or what significance do they have to you personally? Can you identify anything you might believe that is not in harmony with the Bible? Can you identify anything you desire that is not in harmony with the Bible? What are your hopes and dreams for the future? Are these dreams in keeping with God's priorities? Are you willing to face and confess any sinful reactions that have occurred in response to your difficulties? What information in the book has been most helpful to you so far? Can you identify ways God is already working in your heart and life as a result of your willingness to read and consider the truths discussed in this book? After you answer these questions, continue to complete application one before going on to the next concept.

Look!

Set your focus on the good kinds of outcome that will come out of the trial you are facing, not on the pain of the difficulty itself. Although you do not know at the start how this trial could possibly accomplish good or how you are going to get where God wants you to go, you need to know you will get there if you walk along with Him day by day. The first book of Peter was written to suffering believers who faced horrendous problems. Peter could not tell them how God would specifically sustain each of them or where God would lead each one. What he could tell them about the future was that their present suffering had a purpose and a great reward, both in this life and in the next. He shows them that there is a reason behind suffering, that there is grace and strength in the midst of it, and that there is a reward ahead of it. We might not know the road, but we do know the destination. Throughout the book of Peter, suffering believers are urged to look up, not within, to look forward to the purpose and future rewards, not at the present suffering. There is an end, and there is a destination you will come to; therefore, it is important to make wise decisions today that will not be regretted around the bend tomorrow.

Listen!

Once you are able to begin identifying possible problems that are giving you difficulty, you will be able to begin looking for scriptural solutions and specific truths that will comfort you. The Bible has the answers you need, if you will first define the problem the way the Bible does and then look for biblical direction to deal with it righteously. If you are working with a mature Christian friend, pastor, or counselor, it will be immensely helpful if you will take the time to discuss how the Bible specifically addresses each of the problems you have identified. Take notes in your notebook as you listen to your teacher or counselor, so you can review and meditate on key points you will want to remember later.

Remember, if you genuinely desire God's solution to these problems, you must honestly desire a *biblical* solution. Every response and every solution must be both ethical and biblical if God's blessing is to be upon it. If the proposed solution doesn't pass this criterion, it must be rejected. God *always* prepares a way of escape in every trial, and it is *never* unbiblical or unethical in any way! If you agree to this, then ask yourself if you are looking for a solution that has no cost or inconvenience. Are you willing to make a significant investment of time and effort to deal with this righteously? Few depression situations are quick and easy to resolve. In fact, some require very long-term endurance and commitment. You will be greatly helped if you enlist the support of a trusted counselor or friend that is willing to travel the bumpy road with you as you follow God's road map to restored joy.

Go!

Once you know where you are headed and have assessed the situation as honestly as you are able, proceed to embark on a spiritual journey that will take you through the storm and end when you see the clouds roll away and the sun beginning to shine once more. If you are able to discipline yourself to bite off as much as you can chew one little bit at a time until you finish all the applications, then get started on your own. If, however, you are struggling to get through the day, enlist the help of someone who is willing to come along side of you and work with you and encourage you to keep going.

It may be helpful to stay with someone who understands what you are going through for this purpose, or to have someone stay with you on a 24-hour basis to help keep your life orderly and structured in a way that will keep you productively fulfilling responsibilities and moving forward until you are able to do so on your own. Include in your day brisk walks or exercise in which you sustain your heart rate for thirty minutes or more. This will greatly assist your body in its work to restore your body chemistry naturally. Exercise causes your body to produce natural endorphins that provide a sense of well being and calm. Activity and laughter are God's built in anti-depressants; and best of all, they come free of charge with no side effects.

APPLICATION #1—EVALUATE YOUR SITUATION

- ☐ Loss
- ☐ Personal failures
- ☐ Unresolved guilt
- ☐ Dissatisfaction with God's limitations, gifts
- ☐ Failures of others
- ☐ Bitterness
- ☐ Anger
- ☐ Unforgiveness
- ☐ Indulgence
- ☐ Indulging the mind in sinful thoughts
- ☐ Avoiding responsibility of some sort
- ☐ Indulging in fleshly desires to excess
- ☐ Neglect of God's Word, fellowship with Christ
- ☐ Environment
- ☐ Ungodly people
- ☐ Disconnected from others
- ☐ Uninvolved in Christian service
- ☐ Unresolved questions
- ☐ Doubting salvation
- ☐ Uncertain of God's will
- ☐ Interpersonal relationship problems
- ☐ Financial hardship

.

- ☐ Oppressive environment
- ☐ Bored, not utilizing talents or potential
- ☐ Priorities out of line with God's
- ☐ Other _____

APPLICATION #2—GRACE, DEPENDENCE, AND SELF-CONTROL

Depression is often rooted in the awareness, and discouragement, that we are being controlled by our fleshly desires rather than controlling them. Paul expresses the lament of many who find themselves depressed in spirit for this reason. With deep emotion he says, "For I know that in me (that is, in my flesh,) dwelleth no good thing; for to will is present with me; but how to perform that which is good I find not. For the good that I would I do not; but the evil which I would not, that I do…O wretched man that I am! Who shall deliver me from the body of this death?" (*Romans 7:18-19, 24-25*). Paul expresses grief and turmoil in his recognition that his flesh, rather than his soul's desire, so often controls him. Thankfully, Paul does not end this discourse with despair, but in victory when he ceases to depend on his own strength but turns his attention instead to a Redeemer who will empower him to do what is right. Keep in mind that what Paul is discussing in *Romans 7* is NOT his pre-conversion experience. This is a regenerate man who *delights* in the law of God and thus laments over his propensity to sin.

Paul asks who, not what, will deliver him and replies to his own question, "I thank God through Jesus Christ our Lord." This same concept is repeated in Galatians when Paul says, "This I say then, Walk in the Spirit, and ye shall not fulfill the lust [fleshly desires] of the flesh. For the flesh lusteth [wars] against the Spirit, and the Spirit against the flesh; and these are contrary the one to the other; so that ye cannot do the things that ye would" (*Galatians 5:16-17*). To walk in the Spirit is to live in obedience to the Word of God and dependence on the Holy Spirit that indwells every believer. Jesus tells us, "It is the spirit that quickeneth [empowers/energizes]; the flesh [human effort alone] profiteth nothing; the words that I speak unto you, they are spirit, and they are life" (*John 6:63*). The Holy Spirit and the Word of God work in concert together to transform the human heart and empower the child of God with the ability to obey God. The results, or fruit, of this union are obedience and dependence on Christ as partially found in *Galatians 5:22-23*. "But the fruit of the Spirit is love, joy, peace, longsuffering, gentleness, goodness, faith, meekness [humility], temperance [self-control]…"

You need to recognize that self-control, the very thing Paul so deeply desired, is the outcome of your relationship to and dependence on Christ and His living Word. Paul found great joy and victory in this profound truth. Trying harder, exercising more will power, punishing himself, or pleading and crying did not transform Paul's heart or enable him to obey and follow Christ. He learned that we are saved by faith in the finished work and power of God, and we grow in grace by faith in the finished work and power of God (*2 Thessalonians 2:13*). He says to the Galatians who were confused about this truth, "O foolish Galatians, who hath bewitched you, that ye should not obey the truth, before whose eyes Jesus Christ hath been evidently set forth, crucified among you? This only would I learn of you, Received ye the Spirit by the works of the law, or by the hearing of faith? Are ye so foolish? Having begun in the Spirit, are ye now made perfect [mature] by the flesh [human efforts alone]?" (*Galatians 3:1-3*).

First, recognize and confess that you are no more able to transform your own heart to obey God than the Galatians were. You must exercise your will to obey, but you must also recognize that you are dependent on Christ to empower you to obey, and Christ uses His Word to "quicken" or energize you with His power. Think of it as two wings on the airplane, one called "faith" and the other called "obedience," as an act of the will. Both are needed in order to fly. Pray as David did, "Search me, O God, and know my heart; try me, and know my thoughts; and see if there be any wicked way in me, and lead me in the way everlasting" (*Psalm 139:23-24*). Be willing to confess your sin as God shows you the areas in which you lack temperance, then commit yourself to draw strength from the Word of God as you step out in faith to obey it.

The following self-control worksheet is provided as a means to help you evaluate the areas of temperance in which you, as others, typically struggle. Complete the self-control checklist in order to help you clarify areas in which you need the help of God's transforming power. Do not be discouraged by it! Take it all to the throne of God's grace and request mercy and grace to help in time of need (*Hebrews 4:16*). Commit it all to the Lord and with a willing heart submit yourself to Him as a little child to a loving father. Accept His discipline and comfort as

He begins to answer your prayer and transform your character in spite of yourself even as you daily choose to walk with Him. Keep yourself in God's Word, for it is your strength and power; and keep yourself in the love of God, for it is your encouragement and comfort. Remember that we mature and grow in grace over time, just as children grow and mature over time. Our loving Heavenly Father will not overwhelm you with demands any more than a knowing, loving parent will overwhelm a small child with the same expectations placed on a much older child. God will work in your life as you determine to obey Him, without ever becoming angry or impatient with you and without ever condemning you. We are able to welcome God's discipline because it is always something done for us, not to us; it is always for our benefit; and it is always exercised in love, with no condemnation whatsoever. "There is therefore now no condemnation to them which are in Christ Jesus..." (*Romans 8:1a*).

Food

- ❑ Excessive
- ❑ Insufficient
- ❑ Inappropriate Snacking
- ❑ Inappropriate Sweets
- ❑ Inappropriate Fad Dieting

Sleep

- ❑ Excessive
- ❑ Insufficient
- ❑ Irregular

Leisure/rest

- ❑ Excessive
- ❑ Insufficient
- ❑ Inappropriate

Entertainment/hobbies

- ❑ Excessive
- ❑ Insufficient
- ❑ Immoral
- ❑ Ungodly
- ❑ Illegal drug use
- ❑ Alcohol
- ❑ Tobacco use

Work/achievement

- ❑ Excessive
- ❑ Insufficient
- ❑ Inappropriate

Sex

- ❑ Excessive
- ❑ Insufficient
- ❑ Immoral desires/actions
- ❑ Ungodly use of sexuality
- ❑ Perversions (pornography, self-sex, etc.)

Spending

- ❑ Excessive
- ❑ Insufficient
- ❑ Inappropriate

Speech

- ❑ Excessive
- ❑ Gossip
- ❑ Overly blunt
- ❑ Insensitive
- ❑ Unable to keep confidences
- ❑ Angry words
- ❑ Flattery
- ❑ Other _____

Relationships

- ❑ Excessive attention to
- ❑ Insufficient attention to
- ❑ Tearing down instead of edifying
- ❑ Using for self-gratification
- ❑ Wrong emotional attachments that violate marriage or family relationships
- ❑ Other _____

Emotions

☐ Excessive expression

☐ Insufficient expression

☐ Jealousy

☐ Discouragement

☐ Unrighteous anger

☐ Immoral sexual desire

☐ Sorrow without hope

☐ Happiness in wrong things, motives

☐ Fear of judgment, stemming from unbelief

☐ Other _____

Possessions

☐ Excessive accumulation of

☐ Insufficient care of

☐ Inappropriate objects of desire

Clothing

☐ Excessive

☐ Inappropriate

☐ Dumpy

☐ Unkempt

☐ Sensual (intended to arouse or draw attention to sexuality)

Exercise

- ❏ Excessive
- ❏ Insufficient
- ❏ Inappropriate

Thought life

- ❏ Excessive time spent thinking, brooding
- ❏ Insufficient time spent meditating, thinking
- ❏ Unforgiveness
- ❏ Bitterness
- ❏ Worry
- ❏ Immoral "daydreaming"
- ❏ Other _____

Worship

- ❏ Excessive, externally-minded
- ❏ Insufficient
- ❏ Inappropriate
- ❏ Excessive love of anything, including love of self
- ❏ Insufficient love of God
- ❏ Tithing
- ❏ Serving (using spiritual gifts to help build local church/kingdom of God)
- ❏ Witnessing
- ❏ Praise (singing to the Lord)
- ❏ Bible study

- [ ] Bible memory
- [ ] Prayer
- [ ] Corporate worship (church attendance)

Physically Addictive Self-indulgences

- [ ] Drugs
- [ ] Illegal prescription drugs
- [ ] Alcohol
- [ ] Tobacco
- [ ] Excessive caffeine
- [ ] Excessive sugar
- [ ] Adrenaline addiction (induced by dangerous physical activities)

APPLICATION #3—THE NECESSITY OF SALVATION

Now that you have a list of areas to begin working from, you will need to divide the list into two categories. The first category will be problems that are unchangeable. Next to these, mark a *U*, or use a colored highlighter to separate them from the others. The second category will consist of those problems you *can* change by God's grace. Next to these, mark a *C*, or use a different color highlighter to separate them from the others. From your list of *changeable* problems, choose the ones that involve a sinful choice on your part and write them in a separate, new list Finally, reorganize the changeable problem list, listing them in priority of importance to you.

Let's begin with those problems you have identified as being sinful in some way. Later we will address those that may not necessarily involve sinful choices as well as those that are the "unchanageables" in your life. First, however, it is important that you learn how to continue on your journey without having to carry the heavy burden of guilt caused by sin or fears you have sinned in some way.

If you are having difficulty with doubts of your salvation or have any question whatsoever about salvation, stop here to deal with this one issue alone until it is settled in your heart. It is not possible to resolve guilt biblically until you are certain you are a child of God. In the appendix is a book insert called *SavedWithout a Doubt*. Pray, asking God to teach you and give you understanding, then read this carefully. When you are done reading, ask God to show you the reason you are having difficulty with doubt. Following are several problems that may be responsible, including the possibility you have not yet fully understood salvation and simply need to be saved the Bible way.

- Lack of assurance almost always involves the choice to exalt personal experience and our subjective responses to (or evaluation of) truth over setting our mind on objective, unchanging saving and sanctifying propositional truth that is found in God's Word alone.

- Doubts of salvation may be caused by unconfessed sin in the life of the believer. In this case, the believer needs a better understanding of sin's consequences, fear of God, help with understanding and seeking repentance and assurance of God's forgiveness (*Psalm119:9*).

- Doubts may be caused by stunted spiritual growth, which is likely caused by neglecting obedience, Bible study, and prayer (*2 Peter 1:1-9*). This believer needs help with discipleship as a new believer as he learns what the Bible says about spiritual growth and the process of sanctification.

- Doubts may be the result of being young in the faith or lacking in knowledge for one reason or another. This believer usually doesn't fully understand principles of grace (*Ephesians 2*) and greatly benefits from receiving discipleship as a new believer with an emphasis on understanding the process of Christian growth, sanctification, grace, works versus grace, and God's love.

- Doubting may be the result of failure to resist temptations with the shield of faith. Discouragement is a common hindrance to assurance (*Ephesians 6*). This believer needs a better understanding of Christian warfare, resisting temptation, and growth.

- A persistent lack of assurance may be caused by the habitual reliance on inner feelings rather than the Word of God for assurance of truth. This is probably one of the most common difficulties Christian workers face. This believer needs a good understanding of God's attributes and character as well as a higher regard for the power of the Word of God.

- Doubts may be caused by the erroneous belief that one can lose his salvation once saved. This problem needs to be carefully explored with a pastor or competent Christian worker, as it is possible there was never a clear understanding that salvation is by grace alone apart from works. This believer needs to be directed to God's statements, apart from his own reasoning and feelings, to understand that God alone saves and keeps a believer. A biblical explanation of the eternal security of the believer will reveal whether a person is trusting works for salvation and is not saved, or simply has not understood that a believer's eternal destiny and security rests in the hands of God alone (*Ephesians 2:8-9; John 10:27-29; John 5:24; 1 Peter 1:3-5; 2 Timothy 1:12; John 6:39*).

- Finally, a lack of assurance (particularly if it is not accompanied by apparent evidence of a regenerated heart) quite possibly is the result of an incomplete or erroneous biblical understanding of salvation. In this case, one is unsaved, and needs an understanding of the Gospel as well as the eternal destiny of the lost (*1 John*).

If you have not yet settled the matter whether you are a redeemed child of God, seek the help of a counselor at *Iron Sharpeneth Iron Publications*, a pastor, or other mature believer who knows the Bible well enough to help you. Proceed only if you are satisfied that you understand what it means to be saved and have put your trust in the finished work of Christ alone. If doubts have been caused by one of the problems listed above, add that problem to your list. Next to it, write the specific action you will begin to implement in order to resolve doubt. Now, let's talk about how a believer is to deal with sins he commits after he is saved.

Our natural tendency to love sin will be changed by the power of our Lord Jesus Christ when we receive Him as our Savior. To some degree, all believers desire to do what is right and will grieve when they knowingly sin. In speaking about this change of heart that salvation produces, John tells us, "And every man that hath this hope in him purifieth himself, even as he is pure" (*1 John 3:3*). Typically, a believer is painfully aware that he falls far short of the character displayed displayed by Christ, though he deeply desires this kind of character and wants to be changed by God's power.

When the Bible speaks of saving faith, it is referring to something that causes a person to begin living out, or living in accordance with a particular belief. Believing is not mere mental consent. The root meaning of faith always includes action. That which the mind believes, the will must obey. No one spontaneously acts inconsistently with what he believes. If there is no evidence or action that demonstrates a genuine belief, we may conclude that we do not really believe. For example, suppose someone comes into a room full of people and yells, "Fire!" Those who understand the dangers of a fire and understand what the person said may do nothing in response. However, those who understand *and* believe there is a fire will immediately get out of the building. The Bible refers to the fact that faith produces action in *James 2:26*. "For as the body without the spirit is dead, so faith without works is dead also."

A believer wants to be freed from the enslaving power of sin. When he sins, even though he has believed and trusted Christ for salvation, he is typically saddened or discouraged. Part of the problem lies in the fact that we live in a human body that is hindered and contaminated by the effects of sin that came into the world through Adam. The believer is encouraged when he remembers that he will one day be completely delivered from sin's corruption when he leaves this body and is given one that can live sinlessly in heaven with Christ. For this, the Bible tells us, we "groan within ourselves, waiting for the adoption, to wit, the redemption of our body" *(Romans 8:23)*. Meanwhile, while we are subjected to the effects of sin in this world, both outside of ourselves and within, God has provided the means for us to deal with sin and sin's discouragement. Our joy and our challenge, then, is to learn *how* to deal with our human frailties and *how* to appropriate the resources we have as Christ's beloved children so that we can live triumphantly by faith.

Before salvation, we may have recognized right and wrong to some degree and learned to avoid wrong because of its unpleasant consequences. However, our minds were not awakened to understand or respond to God's love or God's commandments apart from how it might benefit us personally. The moment we believed the Gospel and trusted Christ for forgiveness of sin, we were given new life spiritually. Whereas we once could not respond to God any more than a dead person can respond to one who is alive, we are now brought to life spiritually and given the ability to fellowship with Christ as well as choose to live in freedom from the bondage and power of sin that Christ made possible when He purchased us with His own blood.

> *Ephesians 2:1-3*—And you hath he quickened [made alive], who were dead in trespasses and sins; wherein in time past ye walked [lived] according to the course of this world, according to the prince of the power of the air, the spirit that now worketh in the children of disobedience: among whom also we all had our conversation [behavior] in times past in the lusts [desires] of our flesh [human nature], fulfilling the desires of the flesh and of the mind; and were by nature the children of wrath, even as others.

Because we are redeemed children of God, we are not powerless against the enslaving nature of sin. Christ redeemed us from the penalty of sin (eternal death) *and* the power of sin and has given us everything we need to enable us to live a godly life. Notice how we have this power—through knowledge of Christ and through appropriating the promises in His Word.

> *2 Peter 1:3-4*—According as his divine power hath given unto us all things that pertain unto life and godliness, through the knowledge of him that hath called us to glory and virtue: whereby are given unto us exceeding great and precious promises: that by these ye might be partakers of the divine nature, having escaped the corruption that is in the world through lust.

Perhaps the following passage of Scripture will make much more sense to you given a better understanding of the transformation that takes place silently and miraculously at salvation.

Romans 6:12-14—Let not sin therefore reign in your mortal body, that ye should obey it in the lusts thereof. Neither yield ye your members as instruments of unrighteousness unto sin: but yield yourselves unto God, as those that are alive from the dead, and your members as instruments of righteousness unto God. For sin shall not have dominion over you: for ye are not under the law, but under grace.

The misery and fear associated with guilt is greatly alleviated when we begin to grasp the fullness and reality of our redemption. Our sins and the penalty for our sins—past, present, and future—are nailed to the cross of Christ. We are not condemned because Jesus was condemned in our place, for us. This gives the believer something to sing and be happy about! Over and over we read in the Scriptures that believers are blessed and happy because their sins are forgiven and covered by the blood of Christ (*Romans 4:7*). Judicially speaking, we stand before God thoroughly justified, without sin; and as a result, we have all the rights and privileges of God's children as well as complete access to the throne of God. God loves me because I am His—not because of anything I do. Therefore, I *never* need to fear His rejection. Because He loves me, He will discipline me when I behave rebelliously or foolishly, but He will not reject me. It is to the praise and glory of God's grace, and not to any merit in me, that I am made to be "accepted in the beloved" (*Ephesians 1:6*). My judicial standing with God, however, does not change the fact that I am still living temporarily in this world in a body that experiences the weakness of its mortality and a propensity to sin. What, then, do I do about this? And how is my relationship to God affected when I sin as His child?

Because salvation made me a child of God by adoption, I remain a child of God whether I sin or whether I do not. My place in God's family is not affected. However, as God's child I now have a whole new relationship to Him than I had before. When I sin against Him, my fellowship with Him and my relationship of submission and obedience is affected.

When a child willfully rebels against his parent, it is the child's parent that is grieved and responsible to correct him, not the rest of the neighborhood. When such a child has a change of heart about his sin, he will change his attitude toward his parent, admit his sin, and ask for forgiveness and restoration of fellowship broken by the sin. In a very similar way, God expects His children to deal with sin against Him by recognizing it, admitting it, and asking His forgiveness. The moment we repent and come to Him in this way, God forgives our sin and restores the fellowship and blessings of a right relationship with Him.

God isn't surprised when we sin. He knows we will and has made provision for it. It is a profitable exercise in humility and grace every time we recognize our foolishness and seek our Heavenly Father's forgiveness and mercy. If, however, "we say that we have no sin, we deceive ourselves, and the truth is not in us. If we confess our sins, He is faithful and just to forgive us our sins, and to cleanse us from all unrighteousness. If we say that we have not sinned, we make him a liar, and his word is not in us" (*1 John 1:8-10*). In a far more perfect way than a human parent can forgive, God forgives His repentant child. So then, when we sin, the Bible tells us we have an advocate with the Father, Jesus Christ the righteous, because He took our blame and punishment on Himself (*1 John 2:1-2*). Our responsibility is to humble ourselves under God's hand of correction, seek, and then accept His complete forgiveness. To do so is to receive God's grace and blessings. To refuse is to exalt ourselves in pride and invite God's discipline in our life (*James 4:6*).

An example of genuine repentance and prayer to God for forgiveness and restoration of fellowship and joy is provided in David's prayer of confession recorded in *Psalm 51*. Read it carefully, noting David's recognition of personal responsibility without excuses and the subsequent comfort he receives in knowing God forgives according to His mercy and grace and not according to David's goodness. God is always willing and ready to forgive the moment we turn to Him in repentance (*Psalm 32:5; 40:12; 41:4; 130:1-3; 1 John 1:9; 2:1-2*). Notice the sorrow that is always associated with guilt and the joy that is always associated with receiving God's forgiveness in the following passages: *Psalms 32, 38*, and *42*.

Before going on to the next application, spend some time alone with the Lord. Humbly confess every sinful thought or action that you have listed and are aware of, and ask your Heavenly Father's forgiveness. Make no excuses. God wants you to be honest, not only with Him, but with yourself. Your teacher or counselor may want to provide more encouragement for you in this matter of dealing daily with sin and becoming confident and secure in God's forgiveness. If you are not working with a counselor or pastor, you might want to contact this book's publisher for suggestions of books you might read that will help you further and give you the right perspective of God's wonderful forgiveness. Remember that although admission of sin and confession to God and those we might have wronged is a very unpleasant thing to do, but it is the doorway through which you will find the joys of forgiveness. Christians have the promise of joy after dealing appropriately with sin. You will be encouraged by reading *James 4:9-10* with this in mind. There is nothing more freeing to your spirit than being able to lay the burden of every guilt down at the cross of our blessed Lord, knowing He responds to our repentance with the same joy and love that the prodigal son's father displayed when his son turned from his sin and came home.

APPLICATION #4—GOD'S SOVEREIGN WORK

Sometimes we get caught up in the busyness of pursuing our personal goals and desires in an effort to secure our happiness or the happiness of those we love. When our plans or progress in this endeavor are thwarted or hindered by unexpected trials, we tend to react strongly. We don't like to be hindered or stopped from pursuing what we want. When we are, we tend to either accept or refuse to accept what has happened, depending on how we view such roadblocks. If our main objective in life is to get what we want, we will not be willing to alter our plans easily. If our main objective in life is to become like Christ and fulfill His will for our life, we will take into consideration our need to cooperate with God who is working in us both to desire and to do His good will. When this is our greatest pursuit in life, roadblocks make us aware that there is something much bigger than what we may see outwardly or have wanted; and we willingly choose to trust what God is doing, even if it means changing or giving up what is wanted.

Those who understand God's sovereign right to govern their lives for their good and for His glory willingly yield to His authority. Those who see themselves as having the right to govern their own lives and be their own authority have a difficult time yielding their will to a God they cannot visibly see or understand. The latter group tend to want to pick and choose what they agree with or want to obey and make themselves the final authority when it comes to making choices. Thus, what I like is of greater importance than what God likes and what I want takes precedence over what God wants.

The way we respond when God does not give us what we want reveals how much we understand the concept that God is sovereign. At the end of the word *sovereign* is the little word *reign*. This root word gives us a hint to the meaning of "God is sovereign." God reigns over all the earth. He is subject to no one, for He is the supreme authority. There is no higher power than God. Rulers are permitted to have limited authority in their dominion and, in this sense, may be a sovereign; but they are not sovereign over all. A country may be said to be a sovereign nation, meaning it is a nation that is accountable to none other and ruled by its own authority with the right to exercise control over all its affairs. Nevertheless, absolute sovereign authority over the entire universe belongs to God alone.

When entering into the presence of a sovereign king, a subject would immediately assume the position of one who reverences and willingly submits to his authority. Respect and submission would be demonstrated by the choice of gestures, attitude, words, and manner of the one under subjection to the king's authority and rule. Only a very foolish person would treat a sovereign king with disregard, disrespect, or flippancy because to do so would indicate a low regard or estimation of the worth of the king and invite immediate rejection or worse. A fallible human king who possesses absolute power over his subjects is a dangerous person to offend.

When we enter into the presence of the Almighty Sovereign God, we demonstrate our estimation of His worth and our regard for His authority by the way we address Him, the way we submit to Him, and the way we honor Him. We do not argue with one we hold in the highest regard and trust implicitly. We argue only when we dare to challenge His authority and His right to exercise it at His will. When Job questioned God and expressed his belief that his suffering was unjust, he imagined that he would convincingly argue his case with God if he could only have an audience with Him. In Job's mind God could not be both all-powerful and good if he allowed the righteous to suffer pain and heartache that he did not deserve. This dilemma was problematic in his mind for he reasoned that he could not be faulted for his sincerity or faithfulness to God and did nothing to warrant the trials he was experiencing. Good things were to come to good people and bad things only to bad people. How could God be good or loving if He allowed a man who loved Him to suffer?

When God gave Job his wish and spoke audibly to him, God began, not by giving an explanation to Job, but by asking him question after question that he could not answer. Job suddenly lost his bravado and became silent. God then asks Job, "Shall he that contendeth with the Almighty instruct him? He that reproveth God, let him answer it." Job replies,

"Behold I am vile; what shall I answer thee? I will lay mine hand upon my mouth." God continues to question Job and asks, "Wilt thou also disannul my judgment? Wilt thou condemn me, that thou mayest be righteous?" He then proceeds to show Job the foolishness of his argument in light of Job's inability to understand or do what only God can do. By the time God finishes questioning Job, Job can only say, "I know that thou canst do every thing, and that no thought can be withholden from thee. Who is he that hideth counsel without knowledge? Therefore have I uttered that I understood not; things too wonderful for me, which I knew not" (*See Job 38-42*).

God never gave Job the explanation that he had wanted to hear. By the time He was done speaking, however, Job esteemed God higher and himself lower and no longer wished to question God in the matter. The Almighty was simply worthy to be trusted and His wisdom beyond what a mortal man, however brilliant, could comprehend. How God could be both all-powerful and all good was beyond Job's comprehension, yet Job believed God was worthy of his trust and was indeed sovereign over all and at the same time, good and just. Job simply rested in the reality that he could not comprehend God with the limited powers of his human reasoning.

What began with Job demanding an explanation ended with Job humbling himself in submission and repenting of his arrogance. After God and Job had ceased speaking and Job prayed for his friends who had been so cruel to him, Job's life began to turn around dramatically. It is an Old Testament example of a New Testament principle. "Humble yourselves therefore under the mighty hand of God, that he may exalt you in due time; casting all your care upon him, for he careth for you. Be sober, be vigilant; because your adversary the devil, as a roaring lion, walketh about, seeking whom he may devour; whom resist stedfast in the faith, knowing that the same afflictions are accomplished in your brethren that are in the world. But the God of all grace, who hath called us unto his eternal glory by Christ Jesus, after that ye have suffered awhile, make you perfect [mature], stablish, strengthen, settle you. To him be glory and dominion for ever and ever" (*1 Peter 5:6-11*).

The unseen hand of God is working in ways we cannot see or understand. We see only an injustice done by an ungodly person, while God sees a purpose and plan in allowing the injustice. We see the pain and suffering inflicted by a wicked person; God sees an outcome that will ultimately bless and work together for good. We simply see as a human being sees, with limited perspective. God sees from beginning to end with incomprehensible wisdom and understanding. When faced with perplexing trials or hardships, we have a choice to either trust our own reasoning and understanding, or trust God's. Like Job, we may be tempted to become despondent or angry when we suffer the same sorrows those who reject God suffer. It makes no sense to us, and we wish we could see God face to face so we could ask for an explanation and express the depths of our grief—as if that would convince God that we had a better plan than He. Such a response, however, only lands us in the depths of depression, more confused than ever. When we turn our eyes in faith toward God and simply trust Him, even in our pain, amazing changes begin to take place in our heart and life. We will not be exalted until we first humble ourselves under His dominion—His sovereign right to do as He pleases because of who He is.

After reading about God's sovereignty, answer the following questions in your notebook:

- What circumstances in my life am I having difficulty accepting as something under God's control in my life?

- What words in this narrative describe how God wants me to react to the difficult circumstances in my life in light of His sovereignty and love for me?

- How does *Proverbs 3:5-8* relate to my present situation? What things does God tell me to do in these passages, and what things does God tell me not to do? What is the promised outcome when I choose to follow God's instructions?

- After reading *Psalm 28:7*, what do I believe gave help to the psalmist? Why is the psalmist happy?

- After reading *Psalm 27:13*, what am I instructed to believe in order to avoid the temptation to give up when things become difficult?

- Suggested Bible reading chapters for the week: *Genesis 37,39-50*

- Look for and list the reference to each statement of faith or confidence in God that Joseph makes in these chapters.

- List the reference for each statement of discouragement or despair Jacob made in these chapters. Four times in your reading the Scriptures say, "but God" or "but the Lord" Find and list the reference of each.

- Which three major incidents in Joseph's life probably seemed most "hopeless" to him?

- How did God spare Joseph and make each of these three incidents bearable for him while he was going through them?

- What good actually developed out of each incident?

APPLICATION #5—THE SUFFERING OF THE RIGHTEOUS AND THEIR RESPONSES

If you have ever had to take a toddler to a hospital emergency room for stitches, you know what a heart-rending experience it can be. Such a little one has no ability to understand why he has been brought to such a scary place by his parents, why his parents would permit a strange man to wrap him in something that makes it impossible to move, and then inflict pain by poking him with something sharp right in the place on his head where mommy and daddy have been putting ice. Enduring the baby's cries and looks of desperation and terror while the doctor makes the stitches in his forehead is sheer misery for a parent whose instinct is to rescue and protect his child from harm. The child cannot possibly understand why his parent subjects him to such treatment and does not respond to his cries and pleading to be released at once. The parent, however, knows the stitches are necessary to prevent a ghastly scar or infection that would occur unless the wound is properly cleaned and closed. Mother and Daddy would gladly trade places with their child if they could, but comfort themselves instead to know that in years to come their baby will grow up and be thankful they all went through this ordeal together. But for now, it's a trial they endure with aching heart.

God, our perfect Heavenly Father, knows the heartache of subjecting His children to suffering when it is the only means to accomplish a desired end, or benefit. He is not merciless or cold-hearted when He hears the cries and pleas of His own and sees their anguish. He comforts and consoles even during a trial, and He then removes the child from sorrow the moment it has accomplished its purpose. He does not delight in suffering, nor does He allow it for any purpose except that it is for His child's future benefit and joy. "For the Lord will not cast off for ever; but though he cause grief, yet will he have compassion according to the multitude of his mercies, for he doth not afflict willingly nor grieve the children of men" (*Lamentations 3:31-33*). Even when God the Father disciplines His child in responseto accomplish through any difficult situation that arises in our daily lives (*1 Thessalonians 5:18*).

When we react towards suffering with anger, we lack adequate understanding of both our own nature and the character of our God. We are much like those addressed in the book of *Hebrews*. "Ye have forgotten the exhortation which speaketh unto you as unto children, My son, despise not thou the chastening of the Lord, nor faint when thou art rebuked of him; for whom the Lord loveth he chasteneth, and scourgeth every son whom he receiveth....Furthermore we have had fathers of our flesh which corrected us, and we gave them reverence; shall we not much rather be in subjection unto the Father of spirits, and live? For they verily for a few days chastened us after their own pleasure; but he for our profit, that we might be partakers of his holiness. Now no chastening for the present seemeth to be joyous, but grievous; nevertheless afterward it yieldeth the peaceable fruit of righteousness unto them which are exercised thereby" (*Hebrews 12:5-6, 9-11*).

Suffering would not be our own choice in any situation. By nature, we avoid any kind of pain or sorrow and seek out ways to avoid them if possible. Certainly, there is no virtue in suffering when suffering has no purpose. God has no pleasure whatsoever in believers inflicting pain upon their own selves for any reason, least of all as a self-inflicted punishment for sin. People who believe they must deny themselves the comforts of society or inflict pain upon their bodies in order to show devotion to God error greatly. We show our devotion to God by believing what He has said and done and by obeying Him. Asceticism presumes God is pleased with human pain and sorrow or accepts a sacrifice for sin beyond what Jesus Christ sacrificed at the cross of Calvary. Nothing could be further from the truth or more arrogant. God does not delight in suffering, and He accepts only the work of Christ on Calvary as payment in full for our sin when we turn to Christ alone for forgiveness and salvation. The suffering of Christ for sin's penalty is complete. It is finished, and nothing can be added or contributed by man to satisfy the payment for sin.

God has a purpose when we are permitted to suffer the same heartaches and pain that our unsaved neighbors endure in this sin-corrupted world. Christ had a purpose when He suffered the indignities and anguish of the cross. The Scriptures tell us that Jesus, "for the joy that was set before him endured the cross, despising the shame, and is set down at the right hand of the throne of God" (*Hebrews 12:2b*). Christ could endure the suffering of the cross because it had a purpose that would bring great joy in the end. We are sometimes perplexed when we come across a passage of Scripture like the one in *Proverbs 12:21*. "There shall **no evil** happen to the just: but the wicked shall be filled with mischief." Unless we take the time to study the passage carefully, it appears that a believer should assume nothing bad or painful would ever happen to him like it might his unsaved neighbor. We understand the statement when we learn that the phrase *no evil* means, "to come to nought," or in other words, *no trouble that comes into a believer's life will come to naught or be without purpose*. The unsaved person cannot make that same claim, for he does not have a Heavenly Father who protects him from trouble and only permits it for a cause that will work out for good every time.

Our response to suffering when suffering cannot be avoided should be one of trust in God, who knows what is happening and understands what we cannot understand in this life. Peter encouraged Christians who were suffering the loss of property and loss of life for the cause of the Gospel to do just that. He told them, "Wherefore let them that suffer according to the will of God commit the keeping of their souls to him in well doing, as unto a faithful Creator" (*1 Peter 4:19*). When we suffer in this world as others, we have the opportunity to glorify God by our attitude and response of trust in God. Our faith rests in God's promises and faithful character, for our Heavenly Father's character does not permit Him to be anything but good and loving. He has promised those who love and trust Him that His power and grace will turn around for good what Satan or others meant for evil. Therefore, we can obey the command, "In everything give thanks, for this is the will of God in Christ Jesus concerning you," because we can always thank God for whatever He is going to accomplish through any difficult situation that arises in our daily lives (*1 Thessalonians 5:18*).

Anger and bitterness develop only when we insist on having our own way and have our focus fixed on what we want rather than what God wants, which is far better. Rather than complaining about the disappointment or difficulty of our situation, we ought to be praying and asking God to teach us what He wants us to learn through the situation, asking Him to draw us closer to Him through the trouble, asking Him to use the trouble for His glory and purpose, and asking Him to strengthen our inner spirit as we turn to Him and His Word for comfort and grace and wisdom to endure what we face. Do you have a list of Scriptures you turn to for comfort when life's storms are pounding? If not, start a page in your notebook called, "Verses That Comfort and Assure My Heart." Here's a few that might get you started:

> *John 16:33*—These things I have spoken unto you, that in me ye might have **peace**. In the world ye shall have tribulation: but be of good cheer; I have overcome the world.

> *Psalms 62:5-8*—My soul, wait thou only upon God; for my expectation is from him. He only is my rock and my salvation: he is my defense; I shall not be moved. In God is my salvation and my glory: the rock of my strength, and my refuge, is in God. Trust in him at all times; ye people, pour out your heart before him: God is a refuge for us.

> *Psalm 34:4*—I sought the LORD, and he heard me, and delivered me from all my fears.

> *Psalm 50:15*—And call upon me in the day of trouble: I will deliver thee, and thou shalt glorify me.

Other passages you might find comforting are *Psalm 4:8; 9:9-10; 29:11; 46:1; 50:15; 55:22; 62:8; 73:25-26; 85:8; 94:17-19; 112:4; 119:165; 147:3; Proverbs 3:13,17; Isaiah 9:6; 26:3; John 14:1; 14:16-18; 14:27; Romans 5:1; 8:6; 15:13; 2 Corinthians 1:3-4; Galatians 5:22-23; Colossians 3:15*

Sometimes, like Job, we will not know exactly what God was accomplishing through a particular trial until we reach heaven and see it from eternity's perspective. Other times we begin to learn some of the benefits that came because of a particular trial. In other cases, we are aware of the trial's purpose immediately. It will encourage you to consider some of the many reasons God might permit suffering in your life. When you are done prayerfully reading the list, write in your notebook some of the reasons you believe God may be using the difficult situation in your life that has brought you to this place of sorrow.

Suffering steers us away from error.

Psalm 119:67—Before I was afflicted I went astray: but now have I kept thy word. Thou art good, and doest good; teach me thy statutes.

Suffering motivates us to draw closer to God.

Psalm 57:1-2—Be merciful unto me, O God, be merciful unto me: for my soul trusteth in thee; yea, in the shadow of thy wings will I make my refuge, until these calamities be overpast. I will cry unto God most high; unto God that performeth all things for me.

James 4:8-10—Draw nigh to God, and he will draw nigh to you. Cleanse your hands, ye sinners; and purify your hearts, ye double minded. Be afflicted, and mourn, and weep: let your laughter be turned to mourning, and your joy to heaviness. Humble yourselves in the sight of the Lord, and he shall lift you up.

Matthew 11:28—Come unto me, all ye that labour and are heavy laden, and I will give you rest.

Suffering teaches us to pray.

Psalm 50:15—And call upon me in the day of trouble; I will deliver thee, and thou shalt glorify me.

Psalm 116:1,3-4—I love the Lord, because he hath heard my voice and my supplications. The sorrows of death compassed me, and the pains of hell gat hold upon me; I found trouble and sorrow. Then called I upon the name of the Lord...

Psalm 61:1—Hear my cry, O God; attend unto my prayer. From the end of the earth will I cry unto thee, when my heart is overwhelmed, lead me to the rock that is higher than I.

Suffering gives us the opportunity to see God's power.

Jeremiah 33:3—Call unto me, and I will answer thee, and shew thee great and mighty things, which thou knowest not.

Jeremiah 32:17—Ah Lord God! Behold, thou hast made the Heaven and the earth by thy great power and stretched out arm, and there is nothing too hard for thee.

Psalm 4:4—Be still and know that I am God.

Psalm 27:13—I had fainted, unless I had believed to see the goodness of the Lord in the land of the living.

Psalm 28:7—The Lord is my strength and my shield; my heart trusted in him, and I am helped; therefore my heart greatly rejoiceth; and with my song will I praise Him.

Suffering is a way God often corrects us.

Revelation 3:19—As many as I love, I rebuke and chasten; be zealous therefore, and repent.

Proverbs 28:13—He that covereth his sins shall not prosper; but whoso confesseth and forsaketh them shall have mercy.

Isaiah 59:1—Behold, the Lord's hand is not shortened, that it cannot save; neither his ear heavy, that it cannot hear; But your iniquities have separated between you and your God, and your sins have hid his face from you, that he will not hear.

Suffering provokes us to judge and deal with sin in our life before it destroys us.

1 Corinthians 11:31-32—For if we would judge ourselves, we should not be judged. But when we are judged, we are chastened of the Lord, that we should not be condemned with the world.

Suffering teaches us obedience so that we will be blessed.

Hebrews 5:8—Though He were a Son, yet learned he obedience by the things which He suffered.

Suffering deepens bonds of fellowship and love in the church family.

Hebrews 10:34—For ye had compassion of me in my bonds, and took joyfully the spoiling of your goods, knowing in yourselves that ye have in heaven a better and an enduring substance.

Matthew 11:28—Come unto me, all ye that labour and are heavy laden, and I will give you rest.

Suffering teaches us to pray.

Psalm 50:15—And call upon me in the day of trouble; I will deliver thee, and thou shalt glorify me.

Psalm 116:1,3-4—I love the Lord, because he hath heard my voice and my supplications. The sorrows of death compassed me, and the pains of hell gat hold upon me; I found trouble and sorrow. Then called I upon the name of the Lord...

Psalm 61:1—Hear my cry, O God; attend unto my prayer. From the end of the earth will I cry unto thee, when my heart is overwhelmed, lead me to the rock that is higher than I.

Suffering gives us the opportunity to see God's power.

Jeremiah 33:3—Call unto me, and I will answer thee, and shew thee great and mighty things, which thou knowest not.

Jeremiah 32:17—Ah Lord God! Behold, thou hast made the Heaven and the earth by thy great power and stretched out arm, and there is nothing too hard for thee.

Psalm 4:4—Be still and know that I am God.

Psalm 27:13—I had fainted, unless I had believed to see the goodness of the Lord in the land of the living.

Psalm 28:7—The Lord is my strength and my shield; my heart trusted in him, and I am helped; therefore my heart greatly rejoiceth; and with my song will I praise Him.

Suffering is a way God often corrects us.

Revelation 3:19—As many as I love, I rebuke and chasten; be zealous therefore, and repent.

Proverbs 28:13—He that covereth his sins shall not prosper; but whoso confesseth and forsaketh them shall have mercy.

Isaiah 59:1—Behold, the Lord's hand is not shortened, that it cannot save; neither his ear heavy, that it cannot hear; But your iniquities have separated between you and your God, and your sins have hid his face from you, that he will not hear.

Suffering provokes us to judge and deal with sin in our life before it destroys us.

1 Corinthians 11:31-32—For if we would judge ourselves, we should not be judged. But when we are judged, we are chastened of the Lord, that we should not be condemned with the world.

Suffering teaches us obedience so that we will be blessed.

Hebrews 5:8—Though He were a Son, yet learned he obedience by the things which He suffered.

Suffering deepens bonds of fellowship and love in the church family.

Hebrews 10:34—For ye had compassion of me in my bonds, and took joyfully the spoiling of your goods, knowing in yourselves that ye have in heaven a better and an enduring substance.

Suffering develops character: wisdom, patience, and faith.

Romans 5:4-5—We glory in tribulations also; knowing that tribulation worketh patience; and patience, experience; and experience, hope: and hope maketh not ashamed...

James 1:3—Knowing this, that the trying of your faith worketh patience.

1 Peter 1:6-7—Now for a season, if need be, ye are in heaviness through manifold temptations; that the trial of your faith, being much more precious than of gold that perisheth, though it be tried with fire, might be found unto praise and honour and glory at the appearing of Jesus Christ.

Psalm 119:72-73—It is good for me that I have been afflicted; that I might learn thy statutes. Thy hands have made me and fashioned me; give me understanding, that I may learn thy commandments.

Psalm 119:75—I know, O Lord, that thy judgments are right, and that thou in faithfulness hast afflicted me.

Suffering redirects our attention from the temporal to the eternal.

2 Corinthians 4:16-18—For which cause we faint not; but though our outward man perish, yet the inward man is renewed day by day. For our light affliction, which is but for a moment, worketh for us a far more exceeding and eternal weight of glory; while we look not at the things which are seen, but at the things which are not seen. For the things which are seen are temporal; but the things which are not seen are eternal.

Suffering conquers our pride and cultivates humility.

Proverbs 13:10—Pride goeth before destruction and a haughty spirit before a fall.

Proverbs 29:23—A man's pride shall bring him low; but honour shall uphold the humble in spirit.

Luke 14:11—Whosoever exalteth himself shall be abased; and he that humbleth himself shall be exalted.

1 Peter 5:6-7—Humble yourselves therefore under the mighty hand of God, that he may exalt you in due time; casting all your care upon Him, for He careth for you.

2 Corinthians 12:7—And lest I should be exalted above measure through the abundance of the revelations, there was given to me a thorn in the flesh, the messenger of Satan to buffet me, lest I should be exalted above measure.

Suffering openly demonstrates and warns of sin's consequences.

> *Proverbs 16:6*—By the fear of the Lord men depart from evil.

> *Galatians 6:7*—Be not deceived; God is not mocked: for whatsoever a man soweth, that shall he also reap.

> *1 Corinthians 11:28-30*—But let a man examine himself, and so let him eat of that bread, and drink of that cup. For he that eateth and drinketh unworthily, eateth and drinketh damnation to himself, not discerning the Lord's body. For this cause many are weak and sickly among you, and many sleep.

Suffering reveals our ability or inability to trust God.

> *Matthew 8:25-26*—And His disciples came to him, and awoke him, saying, Lord, save us; we perish. And he saith unto them, Why are ye fearful, O ye of little faith?

Suffering teaches us how to appropriate God's promises and comfort so that we in turn may comfort and guide others.

> *2 Corinthians 1:3-4*—Blessed be God, even the Father of our Lord Jesus Christ, the Father of mercies, and the God of all comfort; who comforteth us in all our tribulation, that we may be able to comfort them which are in any trouble, by the comfort wherewith we ourselves are comforted of God.

Suffering is sometimes designed by God to change the direction of our life.

> Read about the lives of Esther, Joseph, Daniel, Joseph, Mary,and Ruth. Suffering was used in these people's lives to put them in the right place at the right time so that they might be used of God and receive great reward.

Suffering causes us to be aware of the reality of an enemy who would torment us.

Ephesians 6:11-18—Put on the whole armour of God, that ye may be able to stand against the wiles of the devil. For we wrestle not against flesh and blood, but against principalities, against powers, against the rulers of the darkness of this world, against spiritual wickedness in high places. Wherefore take unto you the whole armour of God, that ye may be able to withstand in the evil day, and having done all to stand...

1 Peter 5:8-9—Be sober, be vigilant; because your adversary the devil, as a roaring lion, walketh about, seeking whom he may devour. Whom resis stedfast in the faith, knowing that the same afflictions are accomplished in your brethren that are in the world.

1 John 4:4—Greater is he that is in you than he that is in the world.

James 4:6-7—But he giveth more grace. Wherefore he saith, God resisteth the proud, but giveth grace unto the humble. Submit yourselves therefore to God. Resist the devil, and he will flee from you.

Suffering makes us understand our human frailty and God's strength and ability.

2 Corinthians 12:7-10—And he said unto me, My grace is sufficient for thee; for my strength is made perfect in weakness. Most gladly therefore will I rather glory in my infirmities, that the power of Christ may rest upon me. Therefore I take pleasure in infirmities, in reproaches, in necessities, in persecutions, in distresses for Christ's sake; for when I am weak, then am I strong.

Psalm 108:6—That thy beloved may be delivered; save

with thy right hand, and answer me. Give us help from
trouble; for vain is the help of man.

Other Biblical Truths about Suffering

- Suffering is evidence God loves us. *Hebrews 12:6-7; 10-13*

- Suffering enables God to ultimately bless us and reward us.
  1 Peter 5:6-7; 1 Peter 4:12-13,19

- God uses suffering to conform us to be like Christ. *Romans
  8:28-29; Ephesians 2:10; Philippians 2:13; Isaiah 64:8*

- All suffering is allowed by God and is in God's control. *Job
  2:10; 1 Corinthians 10:13*

- All suffering can be used for our good and God's glory. *Romans 8:28*

- Not all suffering is necessary. *Jeremiah 2:19; Galatians 6:7-8; 1
  Corinthians 11:31-32*

When Suffering Turns to Bitterness

When we fail to understand how we should view suffering in our lives
or in the lives of others, we often become angry and bitter toward the
seemingly evil circumstances that surround us or others. The following
verses and principles are included for your further study.

Four occasions when bitterness commonly creeps into our lives:
1. When our reputation is damaged
2. When pain is inflicted on a loved one or on us
3. When our expectations are frustrated
4. When others do not live up to our standard of perfection

Kill the roots of bitterness; and the plants of anger, resentment,
and depression will die. *James 3:14; Hebrews 12:15; Ephesians 4:31*

Bitterness becomes hatred, and hatred must be replaced with love. *Le-
viticus 19:18; Matthew 5:43; John 15:18; Proverbs 10:12; Proverbs 26:24;
13:10; 22:10; 25:15; Isaiah 29:19; James 3:14; 1 Thessalonians 5:14*

127

Bitterness is overcome with forgiveness and humility. True forgiveness is manifest when we return good to those who wronged us, when we accept responsibility for our part in the offense, when we have genuine goodwill toward the offender, and when we cease to bring the offense up to either the offender or others. Forgiveness is an act of love, an act of the will, and act of faith toward God. We learn to forgive by forgiving. *Exodus 23:4; Matthew 5:7, 39-46; 6:12; Mark 11:25; Luke 17:3*

Forgiveness means we stop trying to make other people pay for their sins and offenses against us. Forgiving a person requires us to transfer the responsibility for any punishment to God. Bitterness is produced when we assume the right to punish, which we do not have. *Romans 12:14; 1 Corinthians 4:12; Colossians 3:13; 1 Peter 3:9; Jude 9; Proverbs 20:22; 24:29*

Bitterness is produced when we have a negative attitude toward the offender rather than a positive attitude toward the offense. *Job 2:10; James 5:11; 1 Peter 5:6; 4:12-19*

Bitterness is produced when we focus on what we want, rather than what God wants for us. *1 Chronicles 29:11-12; Psalm 75:6-7; 115:3; Jeremiah 18:6*

APPLICATION #6—FACING PROBLEMS
BIBLICALLY AND CONFIDENTLY

Avoiding things that are unpleasant is something we do naturally. Beginning in childhood we learn how to either confront things that are fearful, unpleasant, or hard or avoid them, as is our human nature to do. The more we succeed in confronting our particular problems, the more confident we become in dealing with them as they arise. However, if we aren't encouraged to deal with difficulties or we fail repeatedly in our efforts, we will likely become increasingly more apt to avoid problems when they come up. If we succeed in finding ways to avoid having to deal with problems throughout our childhood, we will unwittingly set ourselves up to acquire a tenacious habit that will extend into adulthood with results that are considerably more painful and significant than in childhood. Just one of those consequences is a lifelong problem with depression.

Children begin avoiding behavior when they put off doing homework, neglect in cleaning their bedroom, avoid saying no to friends, or fail in admitting fault when confronted by parents. Eventually, these children grow up to habitually avoid things that are fearful to them, such as computing mathematical problems, going to college, applying for a job, initiating a conversation, making changes, talking about things that are personal, saying no, or trying something new. Others avoid things that are difficult, such as learning a new skill, reading a challenging book, communicating more effectively, admitting fault, finishing college, quitting a bad habit, or staying on a budget. Still others tend to avoid things that are unpleasant or involve hard work, such as taking a second job in order to pay a bill, finishing projects that require time and effort, cleaning the house, taking care of a traffic ticket, fixing things that are broken, confronting someone with a problem, getting up in the morning and going to work, or putting things away when done with them.

Avoiding difficult, fearful, and unpleasant tasks isn't limited to our daily lives—it also extends into our spiritual lives. Some folks avoid Bible reading, praying, witnessing, getting involved in church, talking about spiritually personal things, admitting sin, paying restitution, seeking reconciliation, enlisting the help of other believers when experiencing difficulty, or talking with a pastor honestly. The more a person avoids having to engage in problem solving or facing difficult situations the more discouraged he will become. Eventually, it becomes such a stubborn habit that a person who is caught in the avoidance cycle will avoid things without even considering that it is not in his best interest to do so. This will lead to habits of covering up, becoming deceptive, making excuses, refusing to acknowledge problems, or blaming others...and this will produce guilt that will only increase anger, depression, and discouragement.

Many people who avoid resolving problems head on become miserable as the things they are avoiding begin to pile up. The housework becomes so overwhelming a young homemaker may not want to get out of bed to face a house that looks more like a war zone. The bills are so behind and disorganized a young man refuses to open a bill that will only remind him that the penalties alone are now beyond his ability to pay. A student gets so behind in his homework he begins to have difficulty keeping up with his class and wants to drop out of school. An unresolved offense eats at a Christian until he begins to avoid a brother or sister in Christ and eventually drops out of church. *One thing is certain: avoiding problems leads to more problems and more severe consequences.* And when consequences become more severe, many people simply find more dangerous methods of coping, such as escaping them by sleeping, using drugs or alcohol, or partying until dawn. Needless to say, a life caught up in such methods of escaping consequences or difficulties soon spins out of control until hope is gone and severe incapacitating depression or thoughts of murdering one's self sets in.

Putting off something we really don't care to do doesn't seem like a serious or sinful thing. We can easily rationalize that we will do it—just not at the moment. We don't categorize it as laziness, since we may be quite diligent doing other things that we aren't likely to avoid—even good or godly things. Women who neglect to clean their own homes may be first to raise their hand at church to help clean the home of an ill person. Men who excel in their careers may work long hours, but neglect their children who are far more important than career advancement. Students may diligently dig into the subject they love and work so long at it that they just don't have time to get into the subject they find distasteful. Those in full-time Christian work often neglect their family or marriage when they wrongly believe the duties they fulfill in ministry are more important than the duties God gives them at home. We all tend to gravitate toward the things we find most rewarding and put the things that we dread on the back burner. And we can all justify our choices by pointing out the many good ways we are using our time, especially if we believe menial work is less important or less virtuous than others things we like more, and especially if we lead a typically busy American life.

Perhaps you are wondering if there is any way to deal successfully with avoidance when it has become a habit so ingrained that it seems impossible to break. Thankfully for the believer, there is no problem or weakness in the flesh that Christ is not willing to help us overcome. He does not ever turn away a repentant sinner who seeks mercy and help. In fact, there is no sin or failure that cannot be forgiven and no problem that cannot be resolved for one who is genuinely seeking God's mercy. "All that come to me," Jesus says, "I will in no wise cast out" (*John 6:37*). Perhaps you are sighing and saying, "Yes, but will He keep forgiving me if I fail a hundred times in the same day? Surely He must get weary of my failed attempts and refuse to forgive me at some point."

Human beings do become weary and impatient, but God does not. If Jesus would tell Peter to forgive a repentant brother who asks forgiveness "until seventy times seven" (that's 490 times for the same offense in one day), certainly He can be trusted to do the same! Jeremiah comforted himself by remembering that "It is of the Lord's mercies that we are not consumed, because his compassions fail not. They are new every morning; great is thy faithfulness" (*Lamentations 3:22-23*). Jeremiah's hope is renewed as he recalls the greatness of God's mercy and the fact that he starts every day new, with a fresh supply of God's compassion, sufficient to see him through the day no matter what it holds. Our greatest hindrance to overcoming habits is not God's lack of patience or discouragement with us; it is our own lack of patience and tendency to become discouraged and unbelieving.

So…exactly what *does* the person do who knows he avoids things that intimidate him or seem unbearably unpleasant? The very first step in the right direction is admitting it is a problem and calling it exactly what it is—avoiding certain kinds of problems rather than confronting and dealing with it. Before you will be able to begin dealing effectively with the avoidance patterns you have, or are, developing in your life, you will need to think about the various types of situations that cause you to be uncomfortable or cause you to avoid someone, something, or some place. It will help if you consider what things are bothering you or causing you to sense that you are failing in some way, or that your life is out of control. It could be a financial situation, a habit that's overtaken you, a bill you haven't paid, or a debt you owe to someone. Other possibilities might include a build up of household chores you've neglected, children who are not being disciplined properly, people you know you need to spend time with, spiritual activities you can't seem to get in the habit of doing, dental appointments or doctor appointments that are needing attention, or a job application you can't seem to bring yourself to submit. Take a moment to list everything that comes to mind in your notebook before going on with this exercise.

Now that you have a careful list to begin working from, look it over and mark those things that you avoid because they are intimidating in some way. Does engaging in this activity cause you to experience a sense of failure or rejection? Do you struggle with this item on your list because you sense you are awkward at it or because it's never become something you are comfortable with? Mark these items in your list with the letter "i" next to them for *intimidating*. Next, identify those things that you avoid simply because you do not like doing them, or like doing other things more. You will have to be willing to be gut-level honest with yourself to do this one. Mark these items with the letter "d" next to them for *discipline*. (Ouch!) Next, look for those things that you are avoiding simply because you do not know how to deal with them. Mark these with the letter "p" for *perplexed*. Everything else, mark with an "o" for *other*.

We're going to work on your list one category at a time, beginning with those things that are intimidating to you in some way. For each item in your list, I would like you to determine the following:

- What, specifically, can you do to resolve or overcome each intimidating item?

- Do any of the items involve sinful behavior of any kind? If so, what specific sin will you confess to the Lord; and if not, how will you reject accepting unnecessary guilt for it?

- What Scripture references shed light, instruct, or encourage you in this area?

- What practical changes can you make in your life in an effort to gain mastery over your behavior?

Marking a sheet of paper with columns for each topic might help you sort through the list more effectively. If possible, I would advise doing this exercise with an experienced counselor who is able to guide you in applying specific principles to the particulars in your list. Since there are so many possibilities and variables, I will need to be rather general in this book; however, a counselor or caring pastor would be better able to provide you with more personally precise and applicable assistance.

Before going on, take the time to pray, keeping in mind that we are not to place our confidence in our own human ability to reason; but we are to be confident in the fact that it is through Christ alone, who strengthens us, that we can do all things. Our God is ready and willing to help us—now we must be ready and willing to seek His help. God often uses means, such as people, or even a book such as this one; but apart from God, neither this book or any other person or thing can deliver you from the power of those things that are distressing to you. Following are some passages of Scripture to encourage you to remember where your wisdom and strength will come from and to seek wisdom and strength from Him now.

Psalm 146:3-5—Put not your trust in princes, nor in the son of man, in whom there is no help. Happy is he that hath the God of Jacob for his help, whose hope is in the LORD his God.

2 Corinthians 2:14—Now thanks be unto God, which always causeth us to triumph in Christ, and maketh manifest the savour of his knowledge by us in every place.

Psalm 138:3—In the day when I cried thou answeredst me, and strengthenedst me with strength in my soul.

Psalm 118:5—I called upon the LORD in distress: the LORD answered me, and set me in a large place.

Hosea 13:9—O Israel, thou hast destroyed thyself; but in me is thine help.

Look at those things on your list you marked with an "i" for intimidating. These are things that typically cause you to experience a sense of rejection or failure, whether you actually failed or not, or a sense of impending doom. When we are intimidated, we may assume that we fear something to some degree. Generally, we fear people if we believe they might attack, oppress, or threaten us in some way. Most commonly, our "people" fears are triggered when we anticipate being thought of unfavorably, humiliated, rejected, ridiculed, or despised. The Bible refers to this kind of fear as a "fear of man," and indicates that it is a human problem inherent in all of us to some degree. To the extent that we fear man, we will experience corresponding torment and misery. The Bible tells us, "The fear of man bringeth a snare: but whoso putteth his trust in the LORD shall be safe" (Proverbs 29:25).

If our confidence and sense of joy are determined by what people think of us or how people accept or love us, we will naturally be extremely desirous of their approval and increasingly more fearful of their disapproval. In fact, our life focus will primarily center itself on winning any kind of evidence that we are esteemed and valued by others. On a "good" day, when we have received a sufficient amount of approval, commendations, admiration, or affection, our happiness and confidence levels soar. However, on a "bad" day when we are largely ignored or treated poorly, our happiness and confidence levels take a nose dive and hit rock bottom low unless we get a "fix" of love and acceptance. People and circumstances, then, control our life—not the truth contained in God's Word.

Caught in this kind of mindset, people work feverishly to get the circumstances and people in their life to conform to their expectations. Desires and blessings soon escalate to become perceived "needs" that one cannot live without and therefore, are transformed into demands that have become conditions to happiness. Such a life is conformed around winning the love and approval of others at the expense of ignoring God and seeking to please Him above all else. Before long, anything that triggers the anticipation of potential failure or rejection produces great anxiety and a desire to avoid it at all costs. As a result, this person will be rendered less and less capable of responding to God without fear. Spiritual strength and boldness will elude him, for they are produced only when pleasing God, rather than ourself, is our highest priority and delight.

The Bible calls this sense of adoration, submission, and reverent regard for God the "fear of God." The fear of God is the only antidote to the fear of man. In fact, to the degree we fear man, we will not fear God; and to the degree we fear God, we will not fear man. One naturally replaces the other. This is why those who fear man are contrasted with those who put their trust in the Lord in Proverbs 29:25 and many other similar passages. David enthusiastically exclaimed, "Oh how great is thy goodness, which thou hast laid up for them that fear thee; which thou hast wrought for them that trust in thee before the sons of men!" (Psalm 31:19).

"Fear not" is an oft-repeated and comforting command given to believers facing all kinds of frightening situations in the Word of God. Some found comfort in these loving words while others chose not to believe them. Paul faced numerous fears and trials and admitted, "our flesh had no rest, but we were troubled on every side; without were fightings, within were fears." At the same time, his reasonable and normal human fears were put in the context of his confidence in God's sovereign control and his recognition that God gives appropriate deliverance and comfort in every trial. So in the same passage Paul also exclaims, "I am exceeding joyful in all our tribulation." He goes on to describe how God had specifically comforted them (*2 Corinthians 7:4-6*). Paul's priorities were right; therefore, he was able to rest confidently in God's care and purpose for his life.

How can a person rejoice and be happy if someone is rejecting him, or worse, deliberately wronging, or persecuting him? It would be impossible, unless he were responding to a specific belief in what God states is true in His Word. The Bible tells us, "Blessed are ye, when men shall revile you, and persecute you, and shall say all manner of evil against you falsely, for my sake. Rejoice, and be exceeding glad; for great is your reward in heaven; for so persecuted they the prophets which were before you" (*Matthew 5:11-12*). Perhaps you can relate to the young believer who heard this for the first time and asked incredulously, "You mean to tell me that God blesses me when people hate me and separate me from their company because I am a Christian or because I want to live for Christ?" Yes, dear believer, as difficult as it might be to believe, God *does* tell us we are not only blessed but have reason to *greatly* rejoice and leap for joy (*Luke 6:22-23*).

Do you believe this? A good test that will reveal how much you believe this is true is how you respond to mistreatment. Is your first thought at that moment centered on how blessed you are? Are you rejoicing because you are counted worthy to suffer as a Christian? Are you leaping for joy because you just received a reward in heaven? How about the command in *1 Thessalonians 5:18* to give God thanks in everything… Did you immediately do that when you experienced the grief of receiving a bill you didn't have money to pay? Ah, my friend, we all do struggle with unbelief at times, do we not?

The Bible is filled with statements and commands that we obey only when we choose to believe enough to *act* upon them. In order to believe and obey God's Word, we must be willing to distrust and reject conflicting human reasoning *and* feelings. It's not enough to believe and esteem God's Word very highly if it is not acted upon in every day life. This is why James tells us that we are deceiving ourselves if we hear the Word, but don't obey it (*James 1:23*). The Bible is not the guiding force in our life when people or circumstances, rather than God, are able to determine our mood. Whenever we allow our feelings to take precedence over truth, we are relying upon (trusting) our own selves rather than God.

If you believe the fear of man is crowding out the fear of God in your life (welcome to the human race), make a decision to spend some time studying the fear of God, asking the Lord to impress its importance on your heart. As your read passages of Scripture that speak about the fear of God, note the tremendous benefits and blessings that are promised to those who fear Him, including the blessing of genuine joy. Following is a list of passages that will encourage and enlighten you as you read and meditate on them. After reading them all, select the ones you want to remember most and write them in your notebook. After each verse, write the outcome of fearing God, or a specific truth contained in the passage that is significant: *Deuteronomy 5:29; 10:12; 17:19; 14-20; 31:12; Psalms 25:14; 31:19; 33:18; 34:7,9; 103:11,13; 111:10; 115:13; 147:11; Proverbs 1:7,29; 2:5; 8:13; 9:10; 14:26,27; 16:6; 22:4; 23:17; Ecclesiastes 12:13; Isaiah 29:13; Jeremiah 2:19; Luke 1:50; 2 Corinthians 7:1; Ephesians 5:21; Hebrews 12:28.*

Moving to the next letter on your list—"d," for discipline, something all of us could use a lot more of! Every person's life or job, no matter how glamorous, has its tedious moments. Usually we accept the not-so-pleasant details of whatever we do, and do them because it's a necessary part of life. However, if we have the freedom to make a choice to do or not to do them, and other things we enjoy doing are pressing for our attention, guess what gets bumped? Putting off necessary duties lands us in trouble when things we have avoided begin to pile up, or things that are avoided are an essential part of our life, however loathsome. Avoiding distasteful tasks is something that can easily become an ingrained habit.

Here's a precise definition of the word *habit* according to *Webster's Collegiate Dictionary*. A habit is "a disposition or condition of the mind or body acquired by custom or a frequent repetition of the same act. Habit is that which is held or retained, the effect of custom or frequent repetition." Frequent giving in to a temptation or little self-indulgences leads us to the place where we no longer control the bad habit. Rather, *the habit controls us*. The apostle Paul recognized this danger and tells us, "I keep under my body, and bring it into subjection..." (*1 Corinthians 10:27*). Notice that Paul is choosing to exercise control over his body rather than allowing his body to control him. Paul explained to Timothy that he must take care to exercise [discipline] himself to practice godliness in much the same way an athlete disciplines himself to practice physical skills (*1 Timothy 4:7-8*).

The ability to exercise control over our human inclination to please ourselves requires us to change the way we think. Simply changing what we do doesn't change our hearts or make us desire to please God more than ourselves. Many people who don't believe the Gospel exercise impressive self-control in order to please themselves or benefit themselves in some way. We need to remember that the sinful human heart takes great pleasure in feeling righteous and good—and even more so when contrasted with other people who are behaving in unrighteous, selfish ways. It is nothing short of a miraculous transformation when a believer delights to deny himself *in order to please Christ*. This change of heart begins with salvation and progresses as a believer's desires and beliefs are transformed by God's truth.

Heart-level change involves a three-part process. (See *Ephesians 4:22-32*.) First, the Bible instructs us to put off the sinful old behavior. Next, we must renew our mind by redirecting our thoughts toward a biblical understanding of our behavior and changing how we think about the behavior. Finally, we must put on righteous thoughts, words, and actions. Putting off sinful behavior without renewing the mind—or renewing the mind without putting on sin's righteous counterpart—makes change impossible. All three parts are necessary. It is God's power, not man's will power, which gives us the desire and ability to overcome a habitual sin when we humble ourselves (rely on Him) and deal with the problem the way He instructs us to. (Study *James 4:6-10*.)

David understood that the power and ability to walk with God begins first with a decision of the will, but is also dependent on trusting in God's enabling grace and strength to do so. God alone is able to teach and enable us to walk in His ways. David prayed, "Teach me [*dependence sought*] thy way, O LORD; I will [*the will exercised*] walk in thy truth: unite my heart to fear thy name" (*Psalm 86:11*). Notice how David expresses understanding that doing what is right and pleasing to God involves learning to fear God more. Our way of thinking and rationalizing needs to be replaced with thoughts that are in harmony with God's thoughts. Instead of listening to our own heart and ruminating on our own thoughts and feelings, we need to learn to listen to God's Word and then talk (not listen) to ourselves right! Let me illustrate by listing some common self-focused erroneous beliefs that lead people into many different kinds of habitual self-indulgence and then depression.

- I must have _____ or I cannot be happy.
- A little _____ won't hurt me.
- I deserve a little _____ .
- I've tried to stop _____, but nothing works.
- I'll do it…someday.
- I'm just stressed out – this is how I deal with stress.
- What I'm doing isn't any worse than   .
- It's not that big a deal.
- I'm not lazy; therefore, I do not have a problem with self-indulgence.
- I am a very giving person. Giving people are not self-indulgent.
- If I don't like it or feel like doing it, I shouldn't have to.
- I need this.
- Well, that's just the way I am. I can't change my personality.

139

The wise man tells us the lesson he learns by observing someone who thinks in these kinds of ways. "I went by the field of the slothful, and by the vineyard of the man void of understanding; and, lo, it was all grown over with thorns, and nettles had covered the face thereof, and the stone wall thereof was broken down. Then I saw, and considered it well: I looked upon it, and received instruction. Yet a little sleep, a little slumber, a little folding of the hands to sleep: So shall thy poverty come as one that travelleth; and thy want as an armed man" (*Proverbs 24:30-34*). The undisciplined person has an uncanny ability to come up with an endless supply of excuses in an effort to excuse himself, and an endless supply of complaints when he doesn't have what he thinks he deserves and sees others enjoying (*Proverbs 20:4*).

It only took one look at this slothful person's property to see that it was in great disrepair. The cause wasn't death or illness, but the "one day at a time" indulgences of a man who rationalized, "Just a little sleep won't hurt anything." "Just a little charge on my Visa won't matter." "Just a little piece of pie won't kill me." "Just one homework assignment won't affect my grade." "Just one little peak won't hurt me." It was habitual little indulgences that led to overwhelming problems for this homeowner who was no doubt discouraged. He wanted things, and he wanted the blessings of prosperity; but he wasn't willing to suffer or deny himself little indulgences in order to be diligent day after day. Consequently, his enjoyment of sleep denied him the greater enjoyment of prosperity and self-discipline.

Instead of rationalizing, you need to humbly put aside your human pride to be painfully honest with yourself and God. For instance, you might need to reword "I habitually procrastinate" to, "I am habitually unfaithful in my responsibilities." Instead of telling yourself, "I procrastinate because I don't have enough time to complete projects," say, "I am unfaithful in my responsibilities because I'd rather please myself and watch TV (or something else) than obey and please God by fulfilling the responsibilities He has given me." Perhaps you need to say, "I am unfaithful in my responsibilities because I do not care how my laziness inconveniences or distresses others. I would rather please myself than them!" Instead of blaming God or others for the condition of your life, take responsibility for your own choices and admit that God never gives any of us more to do than we can do (*1 Corinthians 10:13*). He's not a cruel taskmaster! The fault lies with us, who mistakenly interpret our feelings and desires, as well as the expectations of our Heavenly Father who delights in blessing us. "He hath showed thee, O man, what is good; and what doth the Lord require of thee, but to do justly, and to love mercy, and to walk humbly with thy God" (*Micah 6:8*).

We must change the way we look at things if we expect to change the way we feel about things. We must change the way we excuse and rationalize things by recognizing it is an expression of sinful desires and lies that we habitually tell ourselves. Once we are honest with ourselves, and are willing to be honest with God, we are able to happily seek and receive His forgiveness and mercy. Because we humbled ourselves, God pours His grace upon us and enables us to do what is right. Then we set off in a new direction by deliberately choosing to practice doing the right things so that we will learn to replace the bad habits with habits that are right and good. The more you practice responding to sin by repenting, accepting God's grace and forgiveness, and putting on the right behavior, depending on God to change your heart as you practice biblical disciplines, the more you will begin to experience victory over sinful habits. You have God's promise, "Being confident of this very thing, that he which hath begun a good work in you will perform it until the day of Jesus Christ" (*Philippians 1:6*).

Habits require sustained effort and discipline in order to "reprogram" (renew) our mind until the deep ruts a habit carves into our thinking are no longer pulling us into the undercurrent of its grasp. It takes repeating the correct response many times in order to form new and better paths of behavior and thinking. The dilemma this often puts us in is that it takes discipline to become disciplined; it's hard work! This is why accountability and assistance from others who are disciplined themselves, (as well as kind and patient), are so often necessary in order to overcome stubborn habits. Some habitual problems require heavy restructuring of our time and life, as well as a helpful person providing the "coaching" and supervision we need to become disciplined.

Following are some principles and passages of Scripture you will want to write in your notebook and memorize.

- Overcoming a sinful habit requires us to be willing to give up the habit. *James 1:6-8*

- God commands us to depend on the power of prayer to resist temptation. *Matthew 26:41*

- Overcoming temptation may require us to change the places we go, people we befriend, or things that we do that encourage indulgence. *Proverbs 4:14; Romans 13:14*

- The righteous counterpart to self-indulgence is *temperance*, or self-control, which is recognized in Scripture as a by-product, or fruit of the Spirit gained by walking in the Spirit. *Galatians 5:22-23*

The last category separating your list of problems have the letter "p" marked next to them, which indicates you tend to avoid them because they are perplexing in some way. Quite possibly these are problems that seem quite complicated or overwhelming and leave you feeling as though you don't know where to begin. There are really a number of reasons you might be experiencing dread when contemplating problems in this category. A few of the more common reasons people want to run from perplexing problems include a general lack of knowledge that would give confidence that is needed to begin tackling the problem, a tendency to look at the whole scope of the problem rather than breaking it down into smaller more manageablewrong assumptions about the problem's difficulty or possible outcome which make it more intimidating than it really is, a false belief that every aspect of the problem must be understood before it can be dealt with, or that it's useless to begin working on it unless it can be resolved all at once.

Most common of all, however, is the failure to believe God knows all about the problem and has a way of escape prepared for each of His children so that they are able to deal with it successfully, no matter what it is or how impossible it looks. No problem is hopeless for the child of God, and no problem needs to be carried alone. It may seem as though there is no answer and no door in the brick wall that surrounds us, but God always leaves a way for us to escape—a little door for us to walk through if we'll just look for it. Jeremiah experienced perplexity in his difficult problem and felt as we sometimes do, that life has "hedged me about, that I cannot get out" (*Lamentations 3:7*). He discovered God is faithful, however, and is encouraged by remembering God's goodness to those who wait for him and seek him. Paul reminds us that the accounts we read in the Old Testament were written for us as examples, to provide instruction for us so we will respond with faith in times of trouble and perplexity. Then Paul follows this by saying, therefore, "There hath no temptation [trial] taken you but such as is common to man; but God is faithful, who will not suffer [allow] you to be tempted [tried] above that ye are able; but will with the temptation also make a way to escape, that ye may be able to bear it" (*1 Corinthians 10:13*).

Imagine you are hiking in a remote mountain area and have gotten lost. Your food and water is gone; your body aches from carrying the weight of your backpack; and your legs feel like they are going to give out on you. You come to a little dirt road and suddenly see someone who is driving an all-terrain vehicle. He stops, you explain your dilemma, and he tells you he knows exactly where you are going and will take you there. You climb into the vehicle, but refuse to sit down, refuse to take off your pack and put it in the carrier, and refuse to drink the water or eat the snacks that are offered to you. Your driver shrugs his shoulders and just leaves you alone as he makes his way through the winding little road to the other side of the mountain where your car is parked.

Now suppose you start complaining about how heavy your pack is, how tired your legs feel, how thirsty you are, and how worried you are because you don't know where you are and have never been this way before. Wouldn't it be fair to say you were making a deliberate choice not to avail yourself of the help offered to you? And wouldn't you agree that your worrying was senseless given the fact that you have an experienced driver and ranger who knows exactly where he's taking you? It's not hard for us to see how absurd and senseless it would be to carry a heavy backpack while riding in a truck and then worry about where you're going. Yet we do the equivalent of this when we carry our heavy burdens even though Jesus tells us to cast all our care upon Him, and we worry about where we're going when the Lord promises He is guiding us and knows the way perfectly. God provides for us, makes a way for us, carries our burden for us, takes us by the hand, and then goes with us all the way. We may be perplexed and weary, but He is not.

Face your perplexing problem by first pinpointing what it is and what you need in order to cope with or resolve it. Then ask yourself what resources God has made available to you to help you in your journey. Are there people available who can give you information, encouragement, or companionship as you set out to deal with the perplexing problem? Are there books available that could give valuable information? Are you near organizations that provide services designed to assist you? Do you have family or friends to consult with or help you? Is this a problem that should be dealt with on a judicial level? If a crime has been committed, are you availing yourself of God's provision for dealing with those who disregard others or break laws? Have you enlisted the help of police officers that are ordained by God for this purpose? (See *Romans 13.*) Is this a medical problem? Have you consulted with a doctor? Do you have legal questions that require the expertise of a lawyer?

The Bible tells us that we are to bear one another's burdens and look out for the interests of others (*Galatians 6:2*). Do you have a church family that would like to exercise this privilege if they only knew you needed them? Are you availing yourself of church counselors, teachers, or pastors who are equipped by God to guide and feed His sheep? Pray and ask God to help you find those people who would be able to provide the right information, guidance, or encouragement to you, and then make a list of all the possibilities. Remember that God most often uses means to provide the help you need, so while people may be one of those means He uses, your expectation is in God. Like David, say to yourself, "My soul, wait thou only upon God; for my expectation is from him. He only is my rock and my salvation; he is my defense; I shall not be moved" (*Psalm 62:5-6*).

God will either provide the means for you to resolve your problem, sometimes in ways you never thought of, or else He will provide the grace you need to endure the problem. Whatever God does, however, is good and has a good purpose and outcome if you will only believe Him and trust Him. Ask the Lord what He might be teaching you in this situation that quite possibly you could not learn in any other context. Be willing to learn and grow and lean on God through prayer and a greater knowledge of His Word. Is it possible God might want you to approach the problem by speaking the truth in love, as He commands in *Ephesians 4*? Are the instructions for your dilemma outlined in *Matthew 18* where you are urged to seek reconciliation to the best of your ability? Or perhaps you will find many truths that you can apply to your situation in *Romans 12*. The answers can always be found in His Word, for our God has promised us it is so. "Grace and peace be multiplied unto you through the knowledge of God, and of Jesus our Lord, according as his divine power hath given unto us all things that pertain unto life and godliness, through the knowledge of him that hath called us to glory and virtue" (*2 Peter 1:2-3*).

Following are a list of passages that tell about a Bible character who had a perplexing problem and had to respond to the problem. Notice that some were delivered out of the problem immediately, while others relied on prayer and faith in Christ for strength and grace to endure the problem. You will notice that some of God's examples prospered in the problem, while others prospered *after* the problem. Still others responded to the problem with anger, despair, or sinful methods of resolving it, which always resulted in added sorrow and loss. In your notebook, write the name of the person you are studying and then write the problem they had, the solution they chose, whether it was a wise or foolish solution, and what the outcome was in the end.

Abigail — *1 Samuel 25:1-42; 2 Samuel 3:3*
Esther — The book of *Esther*
Hannah — *1 Samuel 1 and 2:1,21*
Jochebed — *Exodus 1:2:1-11; 6:20; Numbers 26:59; Hebrews 11:23*
Martha — *Luke 10:38-41; John 11; 12:1-3*
Rachel — *Genesis 29:30; 31; 33:1-2,7; 35:16-26; 46:19,22,25*
Rebekah — *Genesis 22:23-24; 25:20-28; 27; 28:5; 29:12; 35:8; 49:31*
Ahab — *1 Kings 16:28-33; 21*
Asa — *2 Chronicles 14-16*
Cain — *Genesis 4*
Daniel — *Daniel 1*
Hezekiah — *1 Chronicles 32:1-19*
Joseph — *Genesis 39; 40; 41:14-16; 43; 45; 47; 50:16-21*

APPLICATION #7 – GOD'S LOVING PROVISION FOR OUR FREEDOM FROM DEPRESSION

Read the following exercise and fill in the blanks as you are directed to do so. Please read the following verses and then stop and continue this lesson.

> "I am the true vine, and my Father is the husbandman. Every branch in me that beareth not fruit he taketh sway; and every branch that beareth fruit, he purgeth it, that it may bring forth more fruit" (*John 15:1-2*).

The term *purge* is very interesting in light of its meaning during Jesus day. The vine dresser made a soapy solution and washed each stem of the vine to keep insects and disease from ruining the vines and destroying the developing fruit. He carefully cut away the branches that were dry and dead so the nutrients from the soil would not be wasted on nonproductive branches but would be redirected to healthy stems that had the potential of bearing fruit. It was a very tedious and painstaking process.

How would you describe the kind of care the farmer has for his vineyard? Write your answer here, now. _____

_____

_____

What does this tell you about the Father's care of we who are fruit bearing branches? _____

_____

_____

Please read *verse 3* out loud. "Now ye are clean through the word which I have spoken unto you." Notice that the passage says that you are clean *through* His Word, not *because* of His Word. Let's look at *John 8:31-36*. Please read out loud *John 8:31-32*, and *36*: "Then said Jesus to those Jews which believed on him, If ye continue in my word, then

are ye my disciples indeed; and ye shall know the truth, and the truth
shall make you free...If the Son therefore shall make you free, ye shall
be free indeed."

Look at the first sentence in this passage. Is Christ talking to unbelievers
or people who professed to be believers? _____
_____

Before going on, write what you think *verse 31* is saying: _____
_____
_____
_____

Do you think Christ is implying that some are disciples, NOT in truth?
_____
_____

What does Christ say is the difference between a true disciple and one
who is not? _____ · _____
_____

What elements of your problem do you think have enslaved you and
robbed you of the freedom of a contented and joyful heart? _____
_____
_____
_____

What is the condition for blessing that Christ declares? _____
_____
_____

What is the actual blessing promised? _____
_____

According to *verse 34*, what does He mean by being "set free"? ____
_____
_____

Does this mean political freedom, financial freedom, or spiritual freedom? _____

_____

What do you think are the marks of a loss of spiritual freedom? ___

_____

_____

Can you see the connection between *verse 36* and *verse 32*? The Scriptures tell us that it is Christ who sets us free through His Word. Again, we see this comparison in *John 14:6*. Are you able to see how Christ reveals how He works in a believer's heart? Do you believe this wonderful promise could apply to your situation?

_____

_____

_____

In these passages, God is telling us that the proclamation of the Word is how we are sanctified, or changed. Judicially we are cleansed, but experientially, we need daily cleansing and care.

Read *John 15:4* out loud. "Abide in me, and I in you. As the branch cannot bear fruit of itself, except it abide in the vine; no more can ye except ye abide in me." What is the difference in the word abide and the word *visit*?

_____

_____

_____

How do you abide and how does Christ abide in you? _____

_____

_____

Look at the next statement in *verse 4*. We cannot bear fruit if we do not abide in Christ. Do you believe this? _____ Do you believe you can bear fruit apart from Christ? _____

149

What is fruit according to *Galatians 5:22-23?* _____

_____

What do you read in this list that would resolve your experience with depression? _____

_____

_____

This passage in Galatians is not the only passage that defines spiritual "fruit." In other places we read that witnessing to others and seeing them trust Christ is a fruit; faithfulness in serving God and others is a fruit of the Spirit; and esteeming others more important than you is a fruit of the Spirit. Even the willingness to be a servant who doesn't get a lot of recognition, praise, or attention but rejoices when others are advanced and recognized is a fruit of God's Spirit.

Would you agree that there are more fruits of the Spirit than are summarized in *Galatians 5?* _____ Now read *verse 5.* "I am the vine, ye are the branches; He that abideth in me, and I in him, the same bringeth forth much fruit; for without me ye can do nothing."

Would you agree that he is repeating this statement about abiding in Him because He wants us to know it is important? What is the difference between what he says about bearing fruit in *verse 5* and bearing much fruit in *verse 4.* _____

_____

_____

_____

_____

So then, can you see that are we dealing with a difference between an anemic Christian and one who is flourishing and very fruitful?

What do you think He is saying in the last part of the verse? _____

_____

What does nothing mean? Can you breathe without Jesus? Blink without Jesus? Can you move? Can you do anything at all without Jesus? Is Jesus that deeply involved with us, or do we do these things all on our own? Let's look at the first part of *Acts 17:28*: "For in him we live, and move, and have our being." Paul is saying to the Greeks that we are totally dependent on Christ. Even the ability to wiggle our fingers is because God enables us to do so. Those who don't know God do not comprehend this. We who believe God's Word, however, are able to marvel at this incredible truth.

What significance does this study have on your Christian life, personally? How can you apply it to your life? What specific decision can you make right now that will reflect your belief in the portion of God's Word that you have studied?

_____

_____

_____

.

APPLICATION #8—THOUGHTS OF THE HEART

Those who experience the relentless gloom of depression often speak as though they are in a battle for their life, with one terrifying catch—the enemy that is pummeling them to death is invisible and elusive. Police fight criminals with an array of weapons designed to subdue crime. Soldiers fight armies with an arsenal of offensive and defensive machinery. Farmers fight insects with a variety of chemicals, and doctors fight disease with an ever increasing supply of drugs and technology. So what does a soul use to fight a tenacious enemy that comes from within and cannot be seen or heard? Paul reminds us that our most important battles are not with people or things that we can see, but against powerful things we *cannot* see. He tells us, "For we wrestle not against flesh and blood, but against principalities, against powers, against the rulers of the darkness of this world, against spiritual wickedness in high places" (*Ephesians 6:12*).

The weapons we are given are extremely effective to the extent they are able to "quench all the fiery darts of the wicked," yet they are often left untouched in favor of things that can be more readily seen. "For the weapons of our warfare are not carnal [of this world], but mighty through God to the pulling down of strong holds; casting down imaginations, and every high thing that exalteth itself against the knowledge of God, and bringing into captivity every thought to the obedience of Christ" (*2 Corinthians 10:4-6*). The weapons God provides are designed for a specific kind of battle with a specific kind of enemy that God identifies for us so that we will not be confused. Keep in mind that these are not just effective weapons—they are mighty enough to demolish the very strongholds that supply and hide the enemy. Who is the elusive enemy that causes so much chaos and destruction in our life? It is our very own imagination, or defined biblically, our human reasonings cleverly disguised as a comrad. It is anything that prevents us from gaining an accurate knowledge of God, and it is every thought that runs loose like a desperate criminal who has escaped confinement. And what are our "secret" weapons? God tells us it is by His power that we overcome as we exercise our salvation, truth, righteousness, faith, prayer, and the

Word of God.

You cannot successfully fight insects with hand grenades, and you can't fight an army with insecticides. Neither can you win a battle that is staged in the mind with any other means than God has given for that purpose. The battle plan is simple and effective. Listen only to the commands of our General. Follow His directions implicitly. Arm yourself with the weapons God has provided for your safety and victory, and then proceed to carry out your mission which is this: Aggressively track down and apprehend every rogue thought that does not submit itself to the law of God. Once the enemy is secured and captive, proceed to build a protective wall around your life with the knowledge of God that can be found in the Word of God.

Begin to commit to memory passages of Scripture that keep the enemy subdued and prevent future attacks. Write each one in your notebook or on 3x5 cards and read those verses every morning as you prepare for battle. Following are a list of suggested verses.

> *Ezra 7:10*—For Ezra had prepared his heart to seek the law of the LORD, and to do *it*, and to teach in Israel statutes and judgments.

> *Psalm 10:4*—The wicked, through the pride of his countenance, will not seek after God: God is not in all his thoughts.

> *Psalm 19:14*—Let the words of my mouth, and the meditation of my heart, be acceptable in thy sight, O Lord, my strength, and my redeemer.

> *Proverbs 4:23*—Keep your heart with all diligence; for out of it are the issues of life.

> *Proverbs 12:5*—The thoughts of the righteous are right: but the counsels of the wicked are deceit.

Proverbs 16:3—Commit thy works unto the Lord, and thy thoughts shall be established.

Proverbs 23:7—As a man thinketh in his heart, so is he.

Isaiah 55:7—Let the wicked forsake his way, and the unrighteous man his thoughts: and let him return unto the Lord, and he will have mercy upon him; and to our God, for he will abundantly pardon.

Romans 12:2a—And be not conformed to this world: but be ye transformed by the renewing of your mind...

Ephesians 2:3—Among whom also we all had our conversation (behavior) in times past in the lusts (desires) of our flesh, fulfilling the desires of the flesh and of the mind; and were by nature the children of wrath, even as others.

Philippians 2:5a—Let this mind be in you, which was also in Christ Jesus...

Philippians 4:8—Finally, brethren, whatsoever things are true, whatsoever things are honest, whatsoever things are just, whatsoever things are pure, whatsoever things are lovely, whatsoever things are of good report; if there by any virtue, and if there be any praise, think on these things.

Ephesians 4:22-23—That ye put off concerning the former conversation (behavior) the old man, which is corrupt according to the deceitful lusts; and be renewed in the spirit of your mind; and that ye put on the new man, which after God is created in righteousness and true holiness.

APPLICATION #9 – GOD'S PART AND MY PART

Psalm 22:24   God will_____ When I_____

Psalm 34:4   God will_____ When I_____

Psalm 34:17   God will_____ When I_____

Psalm 50:15   God will_____ When I_____

Psalm 72:12   God will_____ When I_____

Psalm 86:5   God will_____ When I_____

Psalm 28:7   God will_____ When I_____

Psalm 31:24   God will_____ When I_____

Psalm 54:22   God will_____ When I_____

Psalm 111:10   God will_____ When I_____

Psalm 112:1   God will_____ When I_____

APPLICATION #10 – FINDING GENUINE HAPPINESS

1. Real joy is a _____ from God. *Ecclesiastes 5:19-20*

2. Real joy is the by product of a right relationship and fellowship with _____.

3. Real joy originates in deliberate _____ we make. *Psalm 104:34; 28:7*

4. When David was deeply distressed as a result of severe trials, the Bible tells us that he "_____ himself in the Lord his God." *1 Samuel 30:6*

5. Following are several ways we can encourage ourselves in the Lord and experience joy. First, we can stay committed to learning and studying _____. *Romans 15:4; Psalm 19:8; 119:111, 162; Jeremiah 15:16*

6. We increase our joy by _____ in God. *Psalm 28:7; 63:7; Proverbs 16:20*

7. We are encouraged when we fellowship with _____. *Psalm 133:1; Philippians 2:1-2, 17-18*

8. We are encouraged when we meditate on _____ (*Psalm 104:34*) and remember God's _____ and _____ in the past. *Psalm 63:5-8*

9. We become joyful when we _____ to the Lord. *Psalm 71:23; 100:1-2*

10. Spiritual _____ for spiritual things produces joy. *Psalm 107:9*

11. _____ produces joy. *Psalm 126:5-6*

12. _____ produces happiness.
Psalm 128:1; 144:15; Proverbs 29:18; Ecclesiastes 2:26; Acts 2:28

13. Achievement through hard _____ produces joy. *Psalm 128:2; Ecclesiastes 2:24*

14. Those who find _____ find happiness. *Proverbs 3:13, 18*

15. When we _____ others, we become happy. *Proverbs 14:21*

16. When we _____ kind and gracious _____, we have joy. *Proverbs 15:23*

17. Living _____ produces joy. *Proverbs 21:15*

18. Keeping a tender _____ toward _____ brings happiness. *Proverbs 28:14*

19. Keeping _____ _____ produces happiness. *John 13:17; 15:11*

20. A clear _____ produces joy. *Romans 14:22*

APPENDIX A—SAVED WITHOUT A DOUBT

Can I Know For Sure I'm Going to Heaven When I Die?

There are many things we will never know for sure in this life. Many questions that trouble us will not be understood until God gives us perfect understanding in eternity to come. Yet happily, there are things we *can* know for sure, *today*, which can give us great joy and confidence. For instance, we can know without any doubt what it means to have peace with God, to be forgiven, to be absolutely sure we will go to Heaven when we die. We can know these things because God has given us all the answers and understanding we need to cope with life, to extinguish every fear, and to make us know for certain the way of eternal life.

It's Not a Secret

God has not hidden His plan of salvation from mankind. The Bible tells us that He is not willing that any should perish, but that all should come to repentance (*1 Peter 3:9*). Therefore, God has plainly revealed in the Bible the knowledge we need in order to be saved. In *Deuteronomy 30:11* God says to us, "For this commandment which I command thee this day, it is not hidden from thee, neither is it far off. It is not in heaven, that thou shouldest say, Who shall go up for us to heaven, and bring it unto us, that we may hear it, and do it? Neither is it beyond the sea, that thou shouldest say, Who shall go over the sea for us, and bring it unto us, that we may hear it, and do it? But the word is very nigh unto thee, in thy mouth, and in thy heart, that thou mayest do it."

God hasn't kept the way to heaven a secret. He came to earth to pay the price for our salvation and made it possible for us to become His redeemed and adopted children. Jesus openly walked before men, died before men, and rose again from the grave to demonstrate publicly that He was who He said He was—Almighty God in human form, the promised Savior of the world! God tells us very plainly, "…there is none other name under heaven given among men, whereby we must be saved" (*Acts 4:12*). Jesus said, "…I am the way, the truth, and the life; no man cometh unto the Father, but by me" (*John 14:6*). Jesus alone has the answer to our heart's deepest need.

We Can Know For Sure

There are actually many places in the Bible where God talks to us about assurance of our salvation. In *1 John 5:13* we read, "These things have I written unto you that ye might *know* ye have eternal life…." In *Romans 8:15-16*, God says to those who have been saved, "For ye have not received the spirit of bondage again to fear; but ye have received the Spirit of adoption, whereby we cry, Abba, Father. The Spirit itself beareth witness with our spirit, that we *are* the children of God." Nothing brings joy to the human heart like knowing we are the beloved of God, forgiven and kept safe by *His* power and not our own! Nothing thrills our hearts like *knowing* that God will not condemn us, nor reject us, nor separate us from Him for all of eternity.

Before we are saved, God's Spirit convinces our hearts that there is a judgment to come and that God holds man responsible for his sinful condition. After we are saved, God's Spirit convinces our hearts that we are forgiven and that we are His beloved children with all the privileges and joys that relationship entails. Be sure of this, God wants His children to *know* they have eternal life.

You may be asking, "How can I know for certain that I've been saved and have this eternal life the Bible speaks of?" There are four basic truths you need to understand so that you may know for certain you are saved.

- You must know and believe you are a sinner.

- You must know there is a judgment and price to be paid for sin.

- You must know that God came to earth in the form of man (Jesus) and took the judgment for sin upon Himself.

- You must know it is not enough for you to believe you are a sinner and that Jesus, as God, died on the cross.

Many people know and believe these things but are not saved. God's forgiveness and salvation are only ours when we receive it God's way, on God's terms.

We Sin Because of What We Are

Let's go back and start with the first thing you must understand—We are all sinners. We sin because of what we *are*, and what we *are* (sinners) is what separates us from God. In *Romans 3:10* God tells us, "As it is written, There is none righteous, no, not one." The word *righteous* means perfect, and God is saying there is not one of us who is perfect or righteous enough to merit salvation. If we try, we will discover that we utterly fall short of God's perfection, which is what we need to have if we expect to earn our own salvation. *Romans 3:23* says, "For all have sinned, and come short of the glory of God." Every single one of us falls short of God's glory and holiness, and that holiness encompasses all that the person of Christ is.

Many people mistakenly think if they keep the Ten Commandments, and their "good" somehow outweighs their "bad," God will pardon them and grant eternal life. This is a grave error, for the Bible plainly teaches that "...by the deeds of the law there shall no flesh be justified [pardoned] in his sight; for by the law is the knowledge of sin" (*Romans 3:20*). God did not give us the Ten Commandments, or any commandments, for the purpose of earning our own salvation by keeping them. Rather, God's commandments make us understand that such things as lying, jealousy, hatred, bitterness, lust, selfishness, etc., are violations of God's law— violations of which we are all guilty.

As we consider God's commandments, and honestly assess our lives, we realize we are guilty of sinning against God. No matter how "good" we may think we are, God says there is "none that doeth good, no, not one" (*Romans 3:12*). The moment we compare ourselves against God's law rather than our neighbor or our own ideas of righteousness, we can come to no other conclusion than what God has already declared—all are guilty because all have sinned. God's laws are good, and keeping them is beneficial; but keeping them can never save us from the penalty of our sins. Our good deeds and intentions can never make us pure or innocent. In *Galatians 3:21-24* Paul asked, "Is the law then against the promises of God? God forbid; for if there had been a law given which could have given life, verily righteousness should have been by the law. But the scripture hath concluded all under sin, that the promise by faith of Jesus Christ might be given to them that believe …Wherefore the law was our schoolmaster to bring us unto Christ, that we might be justified by faith."

Payday Always Comes

The second thing we must understand is that there is a penalty for sin. *Romans 6:23* says, "For the wages of sin is death…." Wages are the recompense, or payment, which we receive in return for what we have done. In this verse God is speaking of the recompense that we receive in return for our sins. This recompense is death. The death He is referring to is not the physical death of our bodies, but eternal death, which is separation from God, and torment forever. Those who die in their sins without God's forgiveness and pardon will stand before God and be judged and sentenced according to the law—God's law.

God warns, "It is appointed unto men once to die; but after this the judgment" (*Hebrews 9:27*). We read about this judgment of the unsaved in *Revelation 20:12-15*. "And I saw the dead, small and great, stand before God; and the books were opened: and another book was opened, which is the book of life: and the dead were judged out of those things which were written in the books, according to their works. And the sea gave up the dead which were in it; and death and hell delivered up the dead which were in them: and they were judged every man according to their works. And death and hell were cast into the lake of fire. **This is the second death. And whosoever was not found written in the book of life was cast into the lake of fire."** No words are able to capture the horror and doom of a soul that dies unsaved. Yet with the utmost affection and earnest care, God impresses upon man the way of escape.

The Love of God

The third thing you must understand is that Jesus died in our place. The Bible tells us that, "God so loved the world [this includes you and me] that He gave His only begotten son [the Lord Jesus Christ], that whosoever [anyone] believeth on Him, should not perish [die eternally lost], but have everlasting life [life forever with God in Heaven]." The first part of *Romans 6:23* says, "For the wages of sin is death...." This is very sobering and discouraging news. However, the second part of the verse says, "But the gift of God is eternal life through Jesus Christ our Lord." This is fantastic, wonderful news! God says eternal life is a *gift*. This means that it costs the recipient *nothing*. A gift is given without conditions or strings attached. It is not received because of anything we have done. The gift of eternal life is only received through Jesus Christ and what *He* did to purchase it. Though it costs us nothing, it cost Christ *everything*. God says in *Romans 5:8*, "God commendeth his love toward us, in that, while we were yet sinners, Christ died for us." This means, Christ died in our place—He took the punishment and judgment for our sins that we rightly deserved. Furthermore, He did so because He loved us, not because there was anything good or desirable in us at all.

Earlier we pointed out that no one is justified, or pardoned, from the penalty of sin by keeping the Ten Commandments. That does not mean man is without hope, or without means of being pardoned. God provided a way for man to be forgiven—He paid the price Himself. God says in *Romans 5:9*, "Much more then, being now justified by his blood, we shall be saved from wrath through him." The wages of sin is death—the price of our sin was Christ's *death* on the cross.

Imagine that I received a ticket for speeding 100 MPH down the highway, and you went with me to court. We stood together before the judge, and he questioned me about the speeding. I was caught; I knew I had indeed sped. The judge asked me to enter a plea. I pled guilty. The judge, in accordance to the law, gave a sentence. In this case he ordered me to pay a $500 fine. I began to cry, and say, "But I don't have $500!" The judge replied, "Then you must spend some time in jail." Again I cried, knowing I was guilty and helpless to justify myself. You, standing next to me, spoke up and said, "Judge, I love this person, and I'd like to pay this man's fine." The judge said, "But he does not deserve that!" You answer, "I know. But I love him, and I want to pay his penalty myself and spare him this judgment." The judge then turned to me and asked, "Will you accept this payment for your ticket?" Of course I said, "Yes!" At that point you put down $500, and the bailiff marked the ticket "Paid in full." No one can ever arrest me for that crime again for a legally binding transaction has taken place. The penalty has been paid, and I received it as payment for my violation.

In a similar, though far more dramatic way, we are rightly judged by God to be guilty of being a sinner. The penalty for sin is death. The judge, Jesus Christ, being just and fair must pass down the appropriate sentence. We are helpless to justify ourselves. Nothing good we can do erases the fact that we have violated God's laws. We are guilty. The Judge, however, has pity and compassion. In addition to being perfectly just and holy, He is also loving and merciful. The penalty must be paid. The law must be followed. But the Judge has the power to pay the penalty Himself. In love for the guilty one, He gives Himself to suffer and die in the guilty one's place. The penalty is now paid in full, and so He turns to the guilty one and asks, "Will you acknowledge you are helpless to save yourself, and are guilty of violating God's laws? Will you accept the gift of forgiveness I have made possible? Will you trust me to pay your penalty rather than trying to justify yourself, in a vain attempt to pay the penalty yourself?"

The Bible tells us, "God sent not his Son into the world to condemn the world; but that the world through him might be saved. He that believeth on him is not condemned; but he that believeth not is condemned already, because he hath not believed in the name of the only begotten Son of God" (*John 3:17-18*). Jesus did not come to condemn, because we were *already* condemned sinners. He came to pay the penalty for our sin and to offer eternal life to all those who would believe and trust in Him. If we refuse to acknowledge our sin and plead guilty, if we refuse to believe in the Lord Jesus Christ and trust Him for forgiveness and salvation, then we are left to die in our sins and guilt. We will then stand before the Judge after we die. The evidence will be presented—every idle word, every angry look, every selfish act, every lustful thought, and every sin we ever committed in our life. We will be pronounced guilty, and we will know we are guilty of all God has judged us for. Then we will be sentenced. The appropriate punishment will be pronounced. Finally, we will be ushered away by the angels and cast into hell where there will be no chance for parole, no hope for escape … ever.

Jesus warned, "He that rejecteth me, and receiveth not my words, hath one that judgeth him; the word that I have spoken, the same shall judge him in the last day" (*John 12:48*). How senseless to refuse Christ's offer! How foolish to insist on doing things our own way! How blind to think our life is better without Christ! How sad to love sin more than a Savior who gave Himself to rescue us from sin! Those who would reject the Savior are left to pay the penalty of their sin themselves. They will one day stand before God and be judged for their sins, including their rejection of Christ.

Salvation Must Be Received God's Way

The fourth thing you must understand is how you must receive salvation, for it can only be received God's way—not yours, not anyone else's. Merely acknowledging that the Bible is God's Word, that Jesus is God, that you are a sinner, and that Jesus came to earth and died to pay the price for man's sins does not save you. Many people intellectually agree with these points, but are not saved. Many more people religiously observe Bible commands thinking they will someday be saved because they have attempted to keep them. However, no one is saved on his or her own merit. *No one*.

In *Matthew 7:21-23* God warns, "Not every one that saith unto me, Lord, Lord, shall enter into the kingdom of heaven; but he that doeth the will of my Father which is in heaven. Many will say to me in that day, Lord, Lord, have we not prophesied in thy name? And in thy name have cast out devils? And in thy name done many wonderful works? And then will I profess unto them, I never knew you: depart from me, ye that work iniquity." Notice that these people whom Jesus has spoken

167

of called Him, "Lord." They knew Who He was! Notice they proph-esied, or proclaimed, truth concerning Him. They knew the Word of God! Notice that these people even cast out demons, having compas-sion for others, and did many other good deeds. They were very giving and self-sacrificial. In spite of all this, notice that Jesus ultimately tells them He has NEVER known them. Even sadder, He calls them workers of iniquity and tells them to depart from Him. According to *Revelation 20*, they are lost forever, without hope, without Christ, and without forgiveness.

Now what is the will of the Father that Jesus speaks of in *Matthew 7:21*? It is certainly not doing all these religious things to earn salvation. In *John 6:28-29* we are plainly told by Jesus what doing the will of the Father is concerning salvation. "Then said they unto him, What shall we do, that we might work the works of God? Jesus answered and said unto them, This is the work of God, that ye believe on him whom he hath sent." Those who believe, rely upon, or put their trust in what Christ has done, not in what *they* have done, are those who do the will of God.

Carefully study *Romans 10:1-3*. In this passage we read, "Brethren, my heart's desire and prayer to God for Israel is, that they might be saved. For I bear them record that they have a zeal of God, but not according to knowledge. For they being ignorant of God's righteousness, and going about to establish their own righteousness, have not submitted them-selves unto the righteousness of God." The apostle Paul is speaking to a group of very religious people, yet he says, they are not saved. They are very zealous concerning God. However, Paul points out that they do not yet understand God's righteousness. They are trying to estab-lish their own righteousness and goodness instead. Like the people in *Matthew 7*, they are striving to do good works to earn God's favor and win salvation. They haven't yet come to the place where they realize they are helpless sinners who are not capable of being perfect or good enough to merit their own salvation. They have not submitted them-selves to God's plan, or God's work on their behalf. Rather, they want to live life their own way and be saved their own way.

Jesus explains this rejection of God's way of salvation in *John 3:19-21*. He says, "And this is the condemnation, that light is come into the world, and men loved darkness rather than light, because their deeds were evil. For every one that doeth evil hateth the light, neither cometh to the light, lest his deeds should be reproved. But he that doeth truth cometh to the light, that his deeds may be made manifest, that they are wrought in God." Those who want to live their life their own way and want to be saved on their own terms hate God's truth. They are indignant and angry to hear they are helpless sinners who deserve hell, not heaven. Such people hate to hear that their good deeds cannot save them, or that they are lost and in desperate need of God's forgiveness. They do not want their way of life challenged, because they love their sins and have no intention of turning from them. ·They want to excuse and justify them—not confess them as offenses against a holy God. In short, they want a salvation that allows them to continue living in open rebellion against God's Word while providing assurance they are forgiven and accepted by God. Such obstinacy only insures their continued condemnation and inability to know the peace that true repentance brings.

In contrast, the Bible tells us those who truly believe are those who also understand they are helpless sinners whose only hope is Christ. Genuine belief always produces a change in attitude about sin and a desire to be freed from it. Believing people come enthusiastically to the cross of Jesus and embrace both God's judgment on their sin, and God's offer of forgiveness and pardon. To those who do not claim any righteousness of their own, and those who do not excuse but rather cling to their sin believing it's "not that bad," God has a wonderful promise. He says in *Romans 10:9-10*, "That if thou shalt confess with thy mouth the Lord Jesus, and shalt believe in thine heart that God hath raised him from the dead, thou shalt be saved. For with the heart man believeth unto righteousness; and with the mouth confession is made unto salvation." Those who confess, or acknowledge, that Jesus is exactly who He said He was—God in human form—and those who embrace Him with their heart, believing Jesus died on the cross for their sins and rose again with power from the grave *shall be saved*.

The Bible explains that with our heart we believe, or trust God, for righteousness. Salvation is not simply acknowledging with our mind that Jesus is who He said He is. It is putting our trust in Him, and Him alone, for salvation, and embracing Him with our heart as our God, our Savior and Lord. To those who will receive Christ as their Savior, God says, "But as many as received him, to them gave he power to become the sons of God, *even* to them that believe on his name" (*John 1:12*). "For whosoever shall call upon the name of the Lord *shall* be saved" (*Romans 10:13*). These verses don't say, "might be saved," or "eventually you'll be saved." These verses say, "*shall* be saved." That's a promise from God.

Believing God's Promises Gives Us Peace

Because we know and believe that God cannot lie, we can know and believe what He promises. He has given His promise to save those who trust Him. Jesus said, "All that the Father giveth me shall come to me; and him that cometh to me I will in no wise cast out" (*John 6:37*). Jesus promises that no one who comes to Him and depends on Him alone for salvation and forgiveness of sins will go away rejected. He accepts and forgives anyone who will receive Him as his or her Savior.

Will you acknowledge to God that you are a sinner who is guilty of breaking His good and perfect law? Are you willing to admit that you cannot save yourself or merit salvation through your own righteousness? Do you believe that Jesus Christ was who He said He was (God), and that He died and rose again from the grave? Are you willing to completely depend on Him to forgive you for your sins and take you to heaven when you die? If you can answer "yes" to all these questions, go to the Lord Jesus in prayer and call upon Him to save you. Trust Him completely, and place your confidence in His Word and His promise to hear and to save you.

The Bible says, "Whosoever shall call upon the name of the Lord *shall be* saved." You have the word of Jesus Himself for He said, "Verily, verily, I say unto you, He that heareth my word, and believeth on him that sent me, hath everlasting life, and shall not come into condemnation;

but is passed from death unto life" (*John 5:24*). Notice that our faith and confidence come as a result of hearing God's Word and depending completely on what God has said. We can never have lasting assurance of our salvation if our faith rests on our feelings, on the opinion of others, or on our experiences. Assurance only comes as a result of focusing on God Himself and on His Word and never as the result of focusing on our inward self or on our feelings or experiences. Though you may be timid or doubting, if you have enough faith to come to Christ, you have enough faith to be saved! *John 6:37* assures us, "All that the Father giveth me shall come to me; and him that cometh to me I will in no wise cast out."

Suppose you had enough faith to entrust your life savings to your local bank for deposit. Though you may fear and fret over the reality of your transaction or the ability of the bank to safeguard your money, your fretting in no way affects the safety of your money. You may make yourself miserable with doubting because you can't trust the word of the bank, but the safety of your money in no way rests on your feelings or your fears. Since it is the bank's responsibility to keep and safeguard your money, it remains safe in spite of you! In the same way, God is responsible to do the saving and keeping of your soul when you entrust yourself completely to His care. He will save and keep you whether you fear and fret in the night or not. Paul expressed his confidence in God's ability and power to keep his soul when he said, "I know whom I have believed, and am persuaded that he is able to keep that which I have committed unto him against that day" (*2 Timothy 1:12*). Notice that the power to save and keep is God's responsibility and depends only on God's ability. We are simply to believe.

If you have received Jesus Christ as your Savior, you will find your comfort and assurance in the truths God has spoken. As you grow in your knowledge of Christ and learn how to rely on the surety of God's Word, your faith will grow and your joy will be full! God says to new believers, "As newborn babes, desire the sincere milk of the word, that ye may grow thereby" (*1 Peter 2:2*). Be sure to include a regular time of Bible reading and prayer in your daily routine, and do not neglect to join and attend a church where the Word of God is faithfully preached. Please let us know of your decision to trust Christ. If you have any questions, we would be happy to answer them for you and provide you with the help you need to get started in your Christian life.

Following are several biblical definitions of words related to assurance of salvation. It will strengthen your faith considerably if you will begin your Christian life by becoming familiar with these basic concepts that tend to form the framework for a Christian's joy and confidence as a child of God.

Paul's Prayer for New Believers
Ephesians 3:14-21

For this cause I bow my knees unto the Father of our Lord Jesus Christ. Of whom the whole family in heaven and earth is named, That he would grant you, according to the riches of his glory, to be strengthened with might by this Spirit in the inner man; that Christ may dwell in your hearts by faith; that ye, being rooted and grounded in love, may be able to comprehend with all saints what is the breadth, and length, and depth, and height; and to know the love of Christ, which passeth knowledge, that ye might be filled with all the fullness of God. Now unto him that is able to do exceeding abundantly above all that we ask or think, according to the power that worketh in us, unto him be glory in the church by Christ Jesus throughout all ages, world without end. Amen

Jesus' Prayer for Believers
John 17:24-26

Father, I will that they also, whom thou hast given me, be with me where I am; that they may behold my glory, which thou hast given me; for thou lovedst me before the foundation of the world. O righteous Father, the world hath not known thee; but I have known thee, and these have known that thou hast sent me. And I have declared unto them thy name, and will declare it; that the love wherewith thou hast loved me may be in them, and I in them.

APPENDIX B—ANSWERS TO APPLICATION #10

1. gift
2. Christ
3. choices
4. encouraged
5. God's Word
6. trusting
7. other believers
8. God; love and faithfulness
9. sing
10. desire
11. Wining souls
12. Fearing God/walking in his ways
13. work
14. wisdom
15. help
16. speak; words
17. honestly
18. heart; God
19. God's commandments
20. conscience

APPENDIX C—SUGGESTED READING

The following books may provide further inspiration as you set out to understand and study the application of God's Word as it pertains to depression. Nevertheless, a word of caution before you prayerfully choose books you might like to read. Remember that God may choose to use people, and certainly we ought to be grateful to those who watch for our souls and minister to us faithfully and sacrifically, but ultimately, our help comes from God alone as we put our trust and hope in Him. We are warned, "Put not your trust in princes, nor in the son of man, in whom there is no help. Happy is he that hath the God of Jacob for his help, whose hope is in the Lord his God" (*Psalm 146:3-5*). God will not share his glory with mortal man. He is not honored when we attribute deliverance to a mortal being, for apart from God, we can do nothing and there is no spiritual victory. Should a human being minister to you in such a way that you are strengthened, instructed, or encouraged, remember that even this is by the grace and power of God that He so amazingly uses sinful creatures of the likes of you and me. "But thanks be to God, which giveth us the victory through our Lord Jesus Christ" (*1 Corinthians 2:14*).

Godliness Through Discipline - Jay Adams
Winning the War Within — Jay Adams
From Forgiven to Forgiving — Jay Adams
Peacemaking for Families — Ken Sande
A Shepherd Looks at the 23rd Psalm — Phillip Keller
Self-control — Richard Ganz
Not by Chance — Layton Talbert
Secrets of a Happy Heart — Debi Pryde
Why Am I So Angry — Debi Pryde
Hinds Feet on High Places — Hannah Hunard
Changed into His Image — Jim Berg
Blame It on the Brain — Ed Welsh
When People Are Big and God Is Small - Ed Welsh
Knowledge of the Holy — A. W. Tozer

ALSO AVAILABLE
BY DEBI PRYDE

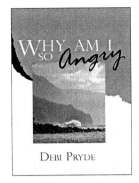

Why Am I So Angry, written for the counselor and counselee, provides a clear definition of anger, a description of the many roots of anger, and a section with personal applications to help conquer anger. Debi Pryde uses biblical principles that move the reader beyond just controlling his anger to conquering his anger.

Abuse is scary and unsettling, whether you are the pastor or counselor offering hope and instruction, the woman facing the abuse in her home, the friend wanting to help, or the abuser struggling to change. *What to do When You are Abused by Your Husband* offers a biblical perspective of hope and lasting peace, concepts often foreign to abuse situations.

The Titus 2 Series, consisting of *The Secrets of a Happy Heart*, *Happily Married*, and *Precept Upon Precept*, is designed to be effective as a personal study book, a group Bible study, a one-on-one counseling tool, or as a Sunday School curriculum. The memory verses, workbook questions, and textual content will provoke thought and encourage Christians to be more Christ-like in all aspects of their life.

Ordering Information:
Ironwood
49191 Cherokee Road
Newberry Springs, CA 92365

760-257-3503
www.ironwood.org